THE WASHINGTON PAPERS
Volume VIII

76: East-West Technology Transfer

Japan and the Communist Bloc

Stephen Sternheimer

Foreword by Amos A. Jordan

THE CENTER FOR STRATEGIC AND INTERNATIONAL STUDIES
Georgetown University, Washington, D.C.

SAGE PUBLICATIONS
Beverly Hills/London

Copyright © 1980 by
The Center for Strategic and International Studies
Georgetown University

Printed in the United States of America

For information address:

SAGE PUBLICATIONS, Inc.      SAGE PUBLICATIONS LTD
275 South Beverly Drive   28 Banner Street
Beverly Hills, California 90212   London EC1Y 8QF, England

International Standard Book Number 0-8039-1485-7

Library of Congress Catalog Card No. 80-50901

FIRST PRINTING

When citing a Washington Paper, please use the proper form. Remember to cite the
series title and include the paper number. One of the two following formats can be
adapted (depending on the style manual used):

(1) HASSNER, P. (1973) "Europe in the Age of Negotiation." The Washington
Papers, I, 8. Beverly Hills and London: Sage Pubns.

OR

(2) Hassner, Pierre. 1973. *Europe in the Age of Negotiation.* The Washington Papers,
vol. 1, no. 8. Beverly Hills and London: Sage Publications.

CONTENTS

FOREWORD

For several years there has been a tug of war within the U.S. government between those favoring stricter trade and technology controls in dealing with the Soviet Union and those advocating business as usual, or, more likely, greater business than ever. President Carter's announcement on January 4, 1980, that, as a result of the Soviet invasion of Afghanistan, the United States would sharply curtail its food and high technology exports decided the issue in the United States at least temporarily. His companion announcement that he would seek allied cooperation in this matter signaled the likelihood that moves to tighten strategic trade controls throughout the industrial democracies would be pushed in allied councils. In short, if detente continues to wither in the 1980s, which seems likely from the way in which the decade has begun, then the subject of East-West technology transfers will be of growing importance, not only with regard to East-West relations but also with regard to politics and economics within the Western camp.

Professor Sternheimer's timely analysis of Japan's position in these matters is, therefore, especially welcome at this juncture. His paper aptly documents the view that Japan does not see export controls in the same light as the United States, namely as instruments of national security and foreign policy that can and sometimes should be used for economic warfare. Although Japan has cooperated with the other industrial democracies on trade controls in the past, it has done so pragmatically, in the interests of Western solidarity and to help maintain the American security umbrella. In the Japanese view, however, export controls are better treated as instruments to promote foreign trade and domestic economic growth.

In addition to this difference in perception, the Japanese, as well as the West Europeans, are suspicious that U.S. efforts to exercise strategic trade controls are part of the U.S. drive to limit Japanese competition with U.S. corporations. Yet Japan sees the development and export of high technology products as essential to its economic growth strategy, and Japan has already become a formidable competitor in some parts of this field. Moreover, current changes in the structure of international production and trade press Japan further in this direction. Competition in low-technology exports from Korea, the Republic of China, Singapore, and other "newly-industrializing countries" and resistance in Western markets to Japanese high-technology products have tended to push Japanese growth and export strategy toward the sale of such products to the Communist world.

The author indicates that Japan seems unlikely to challenge existing levels of trade control, in part simply because no effective domestic coalition for their elimination has yet arisen. Moreover, there is a question in the minds of industrial and government planners about whether it is sensible to sell technology today at the expense of tomorrow's markets in the goods that such technology makes possible. On the other hand, the author believes that there is likely to be little support for, and probably considerable opposition to, tightening existing controls.

Faced with foot-dragging or outright opposition in Western Europe (see Angela Yergin's *East-West Technology Transfer: European Perspectives,* Washington Paper No. 75) and in Japan, how should the United States proceed? The author does not suggest the United States should act in isolation, but he implies that that may be the only option if it does not chart its course on the basis of a careful analysis of the trade-offs concerned. He argues cogently that the United States must be sensitive to its allies' domestic economic and political perspectives as well as to Western strategic interests; indeed, he suggests that U.S. strategic interests may also be damaged by too strenuous efforts to constrain technology transfer on security grounds. His reasons and arguments are essential reading for those who are interested in the increasingly important role that technology transfer seems likely to play in both international economics and international politics.

This volume represents one segment of a continuing Center examination of the character of East-West economic inter-dependence and linkages and their roles in overall East-West relationships. A companion study on European perspectives, the volume by Angela Yergin cited above, is also available.

—Amos A. Jordon
Executive Director
International Resources Programs

INTRODUCTION: HOW NOT TO LOOK AT EAST-WEST TECHNOLOGY TRANSFER[1]

T he world of foreign policy and foreign economic policy frequently appears as a "looking-glass" world, reminiscent of the fantastic landscapes described in Lewis Carroll's *Alice in Wonderland*. In the search for explanations and a logic, U.S. scholars and policymakers alike are prone to "mirror-imaging," attributing to both allies and adversaries those kinds of decisional frameworks and calculations that enter into American policy formulation (Eckhardt and White, 1971). Nowhere is this as evident as in the rapidly growing literature dealing with technology transfer from Western, industrialized nations to countries in the Communist bloc.

Japan stands as the major Asian ally of the United States and as the Pacific anchor of what may be broadly termed the Western alliance. We are interested in Japan's policies toward East-West technology transfers and in the institutional configuration of these policies as they are reflected in export control procedures operating in Japan. We are also concerned with the results of such policies, namely their impact on Japanese trade with Communist nations in general and the way in which they have (or have not) affected the transfer of technology in particular. In the course of our analysis, we will examine the validity of the charge that the process of technology transfer, as it has emerged in the late detente and postdetente period (what Samuel P. Huntington labels Era II in East-West relations), has already resulted in the West's "selling them the rope" as Lenin predicted would happen over half a century ago (Huntington, 1978: 20-22).

The paper also studies the future of Japanese trade relations and technology transfer with the Communist bloc (i.e., the Soviet Union, the People's Republic of China [PRC], and Eastern Europe) from the perspective of this same hypothesis of Lenin's. The analysis focuses on Japanese approaches to national security in the context of foreign policy strategies, her foreign economic policies as they shape and are shaped by domestic economic and international developments, and those factors that have traditionally inclined the Japanese government toward cooperation with the economic arm of the Western alliance, the Consultative Group-Coordinating Committee (CoCom). Finally we are especially interested in the dilemmas that Japanese needs and perceptions pose for the United States as the leading member of the Western alliance—and in the kinds of calculations U.S. policymakers should make to optimize export control policies within an alliance context. With such an approach, we can clear away some of the misunderstanding and misapprehension about the behavior of U.S. allies in the area of export controls and technology transfer. A "rational approach to the subject"—as advocated by Jonathan B. Bingham and Victor C. Johnson in a recent article in *Foreign Affairs* (1978)—surely requires nothing less.

Much of the recent discussion of revisions in U.S. export control regulations—dominated as it is by arguments concerning "acceptable risks" versus "strategically impregnable export-licensing decisions," regulation of "dual-use" materials, and so forth—is largely misdirected. As analyses of the effectiveness of CoCom regulations so aptly illustrate, the rationality or irrationality of U.S. export controls must be evaluated in terms of maximizing intra-alliance cooperation as well as optimizing inter-alliance advantages (Carrick, 1978; Office of Technology Assessment, 1979). The ability of the United States to effectively manipulate technology transfer as a weapon in the interests of national security is not only limited by the availability of alternate Free World sources. It is governed as well by the willingness and ability of other Western nations to control transfers without irrevocably damaging political and economic interests that do not completely correspond to those of their American partner (see, for example, Yergin, 1980).

Recommendations for new alternative strategies to control the transfer of technology per se rather than the end products (as contained in the Bucy Report of the U.S. Department of Defense) tackle only an isolated dimension of the problem (Analysis of Export Control, 1976). The definitional and operational problems encountered by efforts to devise a Critical Technology Approach (CTA) (Davis, 1979) pale beside a second fact: the problem is not amenable to unilateral solution. On the contrary, before the United States can develop satisfactory technology transfer policies, we must know more about how our allies approach this issue, why they do so in this fashion, and whether emerging political and economic forces are such as to incline them along the same or radically different paths in the immediate future.

Our inquiry into the Japanese case reminded us of the maxim that "one man's meat is another man's poison." Interviews with Japanese businessmen and government officials made it abundantly clear that, rightly or wrongly, they regard U.S. efforts to restrict the flow of technology to the USSR, the PRC, or Eastern Europe in the name of Western security as presenting them with a Hobson's choice. Either they are called upon to sacrifice the predictable economic gains of comparative advantage to the uncertain exigencies of U.S.-determined security considerations, or else they must accept a kind of forced technological leveling established through CoCom mechanisms. While they do not question the existence of what R. J. Carrick (1978) describes as "a strategically significant technological gap" between East and West, they attribute it more to the irrevocable domestic failings of Communist systems than to the efficacy of Western export controls.

For the reasons just cited, it is vitally important that more account be taken of our allies' perspectives and strategies regarding export controls in the current policy deliberations over the future course of U.S. trade relations with the Communist world. A clear grasp of such perspectives is critical to the rapid and effective manipulation of such transfers by the United States in response to Soviet-provoked international crises such as Afghanistan and is as important as assessments of the net impact on the economies of those recipients who have become antagonists. Our study will provide the basis for just such a policy assessment in the case of Japan and will develop an analytic framework within which the topic can be broached for other members of the Western alliance.

Much of the information that follows relates to technology transfer between the USSR and Japan. Until very recently such transfers were the most developed and, from the standpoint of a natural market for Japanese technology exports, the most critical. Data has been gleaned from a variety of sources, including interviews with Japanese businessmen, government officials, and executives of trading companies stationed in the United States. All respondents requested and were promised full anonymity in exchange for free and frank discussions. Without their cooperation and generous provision of time and materials, this project would not have been possible. Responsibility for both the analysis and the conclusions, however, rests with the author alone.

I. REGULATING TECHNOLOGY TRANSFER IN JAPAN

The basis for Japanese export controls is the Foreign Exchange and Foreign Trade Control Law enacted on 1 December 1949 (Baker and Bohlig, 1967). In the words of the *Handbook on Japanese-Soviet Trade,* the law aims at "the normal development of foreign trade, and controls the necessary foreign exchange, foreign trade, and other transactions in order to maintain a favorable balance of payments, the stability of the Japanese currency, and the most efficient expenditure of reserves." The principle of export freedom is secured by Article 47 of the law, as modified by the provisions of Article 48, to attain the objectives mentioned above (Nisso To-o Bo'ekikai, 1959: 292-293). Licenses may be required for export at the discretion of the government, depending on the goods involved, the designated recipients, or the mode of payment. Insofar as the latter provision is interpreted by the law quite broadly, i.e., methods other than "standard measures of financial settlement" or cash, the potential licensing authority of the Japanese government under the law seems far reaching (Baker and Bohlig, 1967: 165-166). It is under this provision that the executive branch—or, more precisely, the Ministry of International Trade and Industry (MITI)—is authorized to regulate the transfer of technology to other nations.

The law, however, contains no mention of the control of goods or technology for either military or political reasons. Nor is it specific regarding either areas or commodities for which controls might be invoked. Substantive limitations are contained only in a Government Export Trade Control Order, 89 variants of which have been promulgated between June 1950 and June 1977 (MITI, 1978a: II-B). The order is altered anywhere from one to eight times a year, depending on changes in Japan's domestic economic situation, her balance of payments position, or shifts in the International Strategic Goods (CoCom) list that forms a major component of Japan's national list. The latest variant of the order available contains 204 items.

"Area restrictions" figure in the order's control provisions only marginally. They are not applied to Communist states per se, for the latter are lumped together with market economies under a broad designation "Area A." "Area B" restrictions apply only to those countries for which there are special, non-CoCom embargo provisions (e.g., Zimbabwe) and others (e.g., Iran, Iraq, Nigeria) with whom Japan has had special problems involving the balance of payments.

Several features of the law, the order, and the export control list lend themselves to comparisons with U.S. practices. First, in contrast to the provisions of the various U.S. export control acts (1949, 1969), export controls in Japan have never been designated as instruments of foreign policy, foreign economic warfare, or national security (Brush, 1971; Kitagawa, 1972). By the same token, the positive domestic functions of export control have been spelled out in a way that is absent in U.S. legislation: to promote economic growth, to ensure the stability of the currency, and to develop the economy's foreign trade potential.

Second, both the law and the various orders operate in an atmosphere best characterized by a "presumption of license" rather than "presumption of denial." In contrast to the United States, Japan has never introduced a so-called blanket clause whereby restrictions obtain unless or until a general license is established or validated (Baker and Bohlig, 1967: 171, 174). Indeed, Article 2 and Article 47 of the law foresee the eventual removal of export restrictions entirely by means of a periodic review of each order and through administration of both the law and order according to minimal rather than maximal standards. Further steps in this direction are under consideration. One involves a redrafting of the 1949 law by MITI to reinforce the presumption of license and to eliminate any vestiges of an atmosphere of restriction.

Finally, the list of commodities subject to license under the order is shorter than the commodity control list of the United States. As of 1967, the United States required export licenses for 625 categories of goods, 70 percent of which were not on the CoCom list. By comparison, the Japanese list contained only 194 items (reduced from 203 in 1964), of which all but 17 percent were drawn from the CoCom list. (Others included materials in short supply domestically, products restricted to prevent dumping, and goods licensed to improve quality control) (Baker and Bohlig, 1967: 179-180; Yashiki, 1964: 111-112).

Provisions for the regulation of technology are conspicuous by their absence in the law, the orders, and even printed discussions of export controls. Such transfers, of course, can be regulated legally according to the provisions pertaining to methods of payment. Interviews, however, suggested that they are not. Instead, oral discussions revealed that government officials strongly believe—and businessmen concur—that restrictions on the flow of technology are best left to the normal operation of commercial forces, i.e., the desire on the part of firms to retain competitive advantage. These materials also suggested that the fiscal rather than strategic purposes of export regulation remain quite firmly fixed in the minds of both those administering the law and those subject to it.

In contrast to U.S. rules, export restrictions contained in the law and the orders apply only to Japanese firms located on Japanese territory. They do not govern foreign subsidiaries, branches, or Japanese-based multinationals. There is no concept of extraterritoriality in Japanese trade law—or in Japanese law in general for that matter (except for serious criminal cases). Violation of export controls is a criminal offense, with sanctions of up to three years in prison and a minimum fine of 300 thousand yen (about $1,500 at the mid-1979 exchange rate). If, however, the price of the item involved "times three" exceeds the value of the minimum fine, then the penalty is trebled. Although the law contains no formal provisions for the government to revoke a firm's export privileges, MITI's legal authority to exercise "administrative guidance" in granting licenses means that it can delay export privileges indefinitely in cases of malfeasance.

Written and oral accounts make it clear that export licensing in Japan operates as a consensual process between business and government, not as an adversary procedure. It provokes few complaints, if any, from Japanese businessmen. Most Japanese-Soviet trade (and, since the withering of the "friendship trade" with China in the early 1970s, most Sino-Japanese trade) passes through the hands of 14 or 15 "all round trading companies" (the *sogo shosha*) (Terada, 1972: 434–435; Young, 1979: 195–221). Thus, quantitatively speaking, the Japanese government handles fewer licensing instances than the United States (given large, complex deals involving the exchange of multiple products by trading conglomerates rather than individual contracts signed by small firms). Only a small proportion of Japanese-Soviet trade bypasses these heirs to the prewar *zaibatsu,* and this involves mostly consumer goods handled by co-ops and Soviet firms involved in the coastal trade of the Soviet Far East.

The setting in which the Japanese licensing process transpires differs from that in the United States in other ways as well. Japanese trade with the Soviet Union since its resumption following the 1956 agreements has always taken place within the framework provided by a series of intergovernmental trade compacts. After 1966, these provided comprehensive, five-year projections of all aspects of trade exchanges. Not coincidentally, they also correspond to the time frame of the Soviet five-year plan (Stoliarov and Khesin, 1977: 227–228). (The original initiative for these agreements came from the Soviet side, and since 1968 it has tried—albeit unsuccessfully—to get Japanese negotiators to commit themselves to trade agreements stretching over 15–20 years.) Until the onset of the 1971–1975 trade agreement, each trade plan also included a list of products to be exchanged and estimates of the volume (or monetary) amounts involved. For subsequent agreements no estimates of amounts have been supplied, and the annual breakdowns of both products and amounts have been suspended. The list of items, however, has been retained (Terada, 1972).

The existence of such agreements, even though the Japanese do not regard them as legally binding, affects licensing operations in important ways:

1. *A priori* agreement on what can and cannot be traded exists. Hence, instances of conflict between government and business (and instances of denial) are extraordinarily rare. According to one respondent, the restrictions of the order are applied most frequently to intra-alliance exports (to the United States and West Germany) rather than to those to Communist states.
2. The lists are useful to Japanese companies as a means of signaling favorable market opportunities within the USSR. They also aid in long-term planning by trading firms. In point of fact, the quantities traded usually surpass the levels provided for in the agreements.
3. The lists are credited with shaping the production decisions of export-oriented firms and with "greasing the wheels" of the licensing bureaucracy.
4. Japanese business is protected by the agreements against Soviet dumping. Owing to government involvement and the nature of the agreements, businessmen gain more information regarding Soviet trading opportunities than would otherwise be possible (Terada, 1972).

The licensing process itself is characterized by extensive informal consultation between MITI and the exporting firm even before negotiations with a foreign trade organization from one of the Communist states commence. Companies brief MITI on both the trade package and payment provisions, returning for further consultation if the package alters at successive stages. For exports to non-Communist nations, such a review process operates only when Japan Export-Import Bank credits are involved.

In effect, therefore, a system of preliminary clearance operates to regulate trade with Communist nations. We can only speculate, but it must surely reduce the time, sunk costs, and simple frustration that a Japanese exporting firm experiences in comparison to its American counterpart. At a second stage, the Japanese firm brings the negotiated package back to MITI for clearance of credit and payments provisions—which will also likely involve the Ministry of Finance and the Export-Import Bank. At the present time, about half of all Japanese-Soviet deals involves exporter credits (which were overwhelmingly dominant before 1973 and derive from commercial bank sources). The other half involves buyer's credits that depend on loans from the Export-Import Bank to the Foreign Trade Bank of the USSR.

Our businessmen respondents continually stressed that the major questions from government agencies regarding specific deals did not touch on military-strategic concerns. Apparently, "gray areas" for MITI involve credit and fiscal problems, not security issues in technology transfers. The licensing process is expedited by the fact that the Soviets are flexible in doing business. When they do not think that a license will be forthcoming, they do not seek trade agreements. When a license is denied, there is no evidence of further Soviet pressure. It well may be that American firms are subject to whipsawing in this respect.

In practice as well as law, export licensing remains largely the prerogative of MITI. No interagency boards or committees are involved. The Ministry of Foreign Affairs apparently plays an occasional consultative role, being contacted to "hear its views." The Ministry of Finance is involved on a more regular basis. The fact that security and strategic considerations are minimized in export licensing decisions is further shown by the fact that respondents unanimously attributed an insignificant role to the Japan Defense Agency (JDA) in the licensing process.

Indeed, the primary role accorded economic considerations in export licensing for Communist buyers has given rise to at least one situation where military-strategic considerations—and possibly CoCom restrictions—were deliberately ignored. In the "floating dock case," involving Ishikawajima-Harima Heavy Industries (IHI), the company sold the USSR a $48.6 million floating dock "with a lifting capacity of 80,000 tons, the largest such dock in the Soviet Union" (Mathieson, 1979: 192, 195). In addition to enabling the Soviet shipbuilding industry to carry out more of its own ship-repair tasks than had previously been possible, the sale of a floating dock with a displacement roughly four times as great as that of the U.S. carrier *Enterprise* had obvious military applications. Reports in the Japanese press noted American anger at the failure of the Japanese to appreciate the military-strategic ramifications of the contract which was negotiated in 1975–1976 and fulfilled in 1978. In Japan, after the decision to license the transfer was made, the JDA raised the issue that the dock could easily service Soviet military vessels, given its size and technological sophistication, but MITI allowed the license to stand.

The decision of MITI may have been influenced by domestic economic considerations and the agency's dual mission. At the time, IHI was experiencing economic difficulties. The proposed contract equalled more than half the value of all IHI contracts with the USSR, 1965–1975, and roughly 14 percent of the value of all Japanese maritime-related trade with the Soviet Union during the same decade (Mathieson, 1979: 191). (It is interesting to note that Mitsubishi Heavy Industries, traditionally the single largest supplier of vessels and related equipment to the USSR, is in a similar position today and apparently has given some indication of a desire to export vessels with potential military application to a willing Soviet buyer.)

To cite such a case is not to argue, however, that strategic and economic criteria necessarily point in opposite directions vis-à-vis export licensing decisions. The Tyumen oil development scheme which collapsed in late 1974 and has been officially shelved is a case in point (Mathieson, 1979: 84–92; Hardt et al., 1974: 46–47). Despite the fact that Japanese enthusiasm was always tempered by clear expressions of Chinese concern over the project's strategic implications and by politically motivated U.S. withdrawal from cofinancing arrangements, there is evidence that the Japanese were far from convinced of the economic desirability of the project even in 1974–1975. Since then, the estimated costs of the project have doubled. By unofficial accounts, even if U.S. participation were to be revived and the Stevenson and Jackson-Vanik amendments lifted, the project is economically dead as far as the Japanese are concerned.

In any event, issues of conflict in the licensing process rarely surface. When there are differences of opinion within MITI (or strong communications by one of the other ministries), then

MITI convenes an informal committee that is usually made up of members from the economic agencies (the Ministry of Finance, the Export-Import Bank, Economic Planning) and the Ministry of Foreign Affairs. Only when bank-to-bank loans are at stake is the conflict likely to be passed up to the level of the cabinet and prime minister.

There are no provisions for public accountability in the licensing process. The government is not required to bring instances of approval or denial to the attention of the Diet (the Japanese Parliament) or the public at large. (Although notification of contracts completed is published in an official gazette, information about license approvals or denials is not.) It appears that none of the parties involved view such a system as unduly arbitrary or restrictive. Certainly, there has been no discussion of the issue of export controls, technology transfer, or licensing procedures in the Diet during the past few years (1976–1978).

It is also worth noting that import restrictions do not play any major role in regulating Japanese exports to the Communist world (JETRO, 1978: 4–7, 12–16). Since 1957, the Soviet Union has enjoyed most favored nation (MFN) status in its trade with Japan. East European nations also enjoy this privilege, with the possible exception of Hungary; together with the Soviet Union, they have been involved in Japan's import liberalization measures on a par with other nations. From 1972 onwards, Japan has extended the UN tariff preferences established for less developed countries (LDCs) to three East European nations: Yugoslavia, Bulgaria, and Rumania (Terada, 1972). Moreover, given that Japanese imports from Communist states consist heavily of raw materials and fuels, customs duties play a negligible role in constricting trade. In 1970, fully 70 percent of *all* Japanese imports called for customs duties of at least 10-15 percent (reduced to half of all imports by 1973). At the same time, however, customs tariffs never amounted to more than 6.3 percent for goods coming from the USSR, owing to the large proportion of raw materials and fuels included (Terada, 1972).

The reasons behind liberal trade restrictions with regard to Communist nations are not difficult to fathom. First, and especially over the last decade, the Soviet Union has been recognized by Japan as an important source of the raw materials that Japanese industry requires. In 1975, the USSR provided 20 percent of Japan's lumber and cotton imports, 21 percent of her potassium salt imports, 26 percent of her nickel imports, 39 percent of her asbestos, and between 40 and 80 percent of all precious metal imports. The Soviet Union ranked third in importance as a source of iron ore, chromium, and copper, respectively, and fourth in terms of both coking coal and machinery (Stoliarov and Khesin, 1977: 229). For Japan, each of these falls in an area of high import dependency (in many cases, 85-100 percent) (Hardt, et al., 1974: 44).

Further, by the mid-1970s Japan could import coal from Siberia at a cost of $3 per ton versus $18 a ton from the United States, another major supplier. Japanese oil imports from the Middle East require a month in transit, tankers of 100 thousand tons and 1,000 yen per ton to transport. By contrast, oil imported from the USSR (until the collapse of the ill-fated Tyumen oil project) would have required only two days in transport, tankers in the range of 25-50 thousand tons, and transport costs of 200 yen per ton (exclusive of internal transportation costs from the Soviet oil fields to the port of shipment) (Hardt, et al., 1974: 45; Swearingen, 1978: 121-128). Japanese assistance for the development of the Soviet Far Eastern port of Vostochny in the form of loading equipment, construction, and credits (to the amount of $80 million) doubled the export capacity of that port. In turn, this has enhanced the ability of the USSR to ship such items as timber, coal, and the industrial wood chips used by Japan in her steel, paper pulp, and chemical industries (Swearingen, 1978: 135; Stoliarov and Khesin, 1977: 235-236).

Second, as Roger Swearingen points out (1978: 133), there is a natural complement between the current Soviet need to develop its Siberian resources and the future of Japan's economy: "Assuming the Soviets are moderately sensible about their long-term economic interests and that the Japanese are reasonably perceptive and cautious with respect to their interrelated economic and strategic future, the joint development projects undertaken over the past decade [1968-1978, in Siberia] make a certain degree of mutual sense." Other analysts are less sanguine, citing political obstacles (the Northern Territories issue and the fisheries dispute), alternative opportunities for Japanese capital investment, and the difficulty in using Siberian resources for large-scale fulfillment of Japan's energy needs (Robinson, 1978). Such pessimism, however, may be exaggerated, for it is predicated on a concept of linkage and on the possibility of unimpeded unilateral action that the Japanese themselves reject. As, one Japanese respondent put it, "If we 'link,' then they will 'link,' " and, by implication, both will suffer. Another noted (correctly) that the USSR as a supplier for Japan occupies a relatively more important place than Japan does as a source of imports for the Soviet Union (see Chapter III).

Why, then, has Japan evinced a willingness to adhere to CoCom and to incorporate the CoCom list of embargoed goods into her own list of licensed exports? By developing plausible scenarios for Japan's past actions, we can simultaneously provide a basis for projecting its relationship to CoCom into the short-term future.

In the first place, the assumption that Japan is the preeminent trading nation among CoCom members and is therefore the "weakest link" in any chain forged to shackle or restrict East-West trade does not stand up to close scrutiny. In terms of per capita dollar value of total exports and imports in 1976, Japan ranked only eighth of the major Western trading nations. In order of importance of trade, she fell behind Belgium, the Netherlands, Sweden, West Germany, France, the U.K., and Italy—and she was only marginally ahead of the United States. A similar rank order-ing emerges when we look at the ratio of "the combined exports-imports of individual Western nations" to their "total GDPs (Gross Domestic Product)" (Nippon, 1978: 79).

However, there were a number of forces which propelled Japan into CoCom almost at the very outset. The role of U.S. aid in Japan's postwar economic recovery, the importance of the American political and military "umbrella" for Japanese security, and the psychological dependence bred by the trauma of wartime defeat left their impression on successive Japanese governments until well into the 1960s. Each followed the American lead in basic matters of foreign policy, sometimes under pressure, some-times not. Such factors were reinforced by legitimate security concerns on the part of the Japanese, given the absence of a peace treaty with the Soviet Union, ongoing political disputes with the USSR over the Northern Territories and fishing grounds, and relations with the PRC which were erratic at best. The latter were further complicated by domestic political maneuvering among Japan's political parties, American pressure, and a firm commit-ment to the San Francisco system with all its corollaries (Lee, 1976: 23–82). It should be noted, however, that with the expan-sion of trade with both the Soviet Union and China since 1968, the Nixon "shocks" of 1972, and the diplomatic rapprochement with China in 1978, some of these forces may well have dis-sipated.

Further analysis reveals that CoCom controls may have been acceptable precisely because they did not substantially limit Japan's freedom of action in her foreign trade dealings or domes-tic economic development until quite recently. Japanese-Soviet trade was always quite small, even before any embargo or con-trols. Prior to World War II, the USSR absorbed only 2.0 percent of all Japanese exports and provided only 2.5 percent of her imports—roughly the same proportions that it does today (Swearingen, 1978: 143, 144). The Soviet government, mean-while, whatever its rhetoric regarding expanded trade with Japan, did not make any major commitment to the development of Siberian resources until the mid-1960s. The foreign trade situ-ation vis-à-vis the PRC was somewhat more complicated, if only because a far larger proportion of Japan's prewar exports (21.6 percent) and imports (12.9 percent) were targeted on China (Lee, 1976: 135). But if American pressure to participate in CoCom and ChinCom in 1952 was decisive in rupturing trade relations with the PRC, it is also worth noting that Japan emerged as a direct beneficiary from both the Korean War and her new eco-nomic ties to Taiwan.

Nor, given the pattern of Japanese domestic economic devel-opment, is there any reason to suppose that the nation was straining at CoCom controls in the immediate postwar years. During this period, Japan functioned primarily as an importer, not exporter, of technology in the international trade arena. Between 1950 and 1960, the Japanese purchased approximately 2,500 licenses. (By contrast, the USSR had in force only 250 import licenses at the end of 1972, a miniscule proportion of the 50 thousand plus that one source claims were in force throughout the world in 1969 [Hanson, 1976: 143].) Commodity restrictions were probably unimportant as well. Alternate markets for Japanese goods in Western nations abounded; the spiral of Japanese import restrictions followed by a rising tide of retaliatory protectionism had not yet begun its upward course. Equally important for technology export pressures, Japan still lacked a substantial native R&D effort linked to the production of military goods. As of 1972, Japanese military expenditures were lower than those of the United States, the Soviet Union, West Germany, France, or the U.K. on a per capita basis (Podolski, 1976: 121).

Such explanations for the original trade solidarity of the Western alliance are striking by their dependence on a particular confluence of historical conditions. The fact remains that these are not likely to repeat themselves. How long they are likely to persist—and the reasons why they may already be undergoing important changes—are questions that will be taken up presently. First, however, it is necessary to examine in more detail the outcome of Japanese export regulation in terms of its impact on the size, composition, and trends of Japanese trade relations with the USSR, PRC, and nations of Eastern Europe. Such investigations, together with a study of the comparative importance of Japan as a source of technology imports for the Communist bloc, form the subject matter of the next chapter.

II. THE SIGNIFICANCE OF TECHNOLOGY TRANSFER AS AN OUTCOME OF POLICY

The problems involved in devising policies for the control of technology transfer require more than demonstrations that the asymmetries of East-West trade, plus a failure to appreciate the economic and political costs involved for the West, amount to an unwitting acquiesence to "sell them the rope" by votaries of increased East-West trade (Gershman, 1979). Measuring the impact of technology transfer on the economies of receiving nations involves numerous complexities and subtle but significant distinctions, a discussion of which lies beyond the purview of this essay. A brief summary of some of the relevant issues, however, helps place Japanese behavior and practices—and their significance for the Western alliance—into proper perspective.

First, as the 1976 Bucy Report and the work of the Defense Science Board in the United States makes clear, it is important to preserve the distinction between products and technology (between the item produced and the know-how required to produce it), between critical or high technology and technology in general, and between direct acquisition and reverse engineering (which is less feasible as the sophistication of products and machines increases). Further, as the Bucy Report points out, it is impossible to control technology transfer or to assess its potential impact without some sense of the relative importance of various modes of transfer in terms of ease of transmission and absorption. To put the matter simply, some channels are more equal than others.

From a second perspective, any claim that Western alliance members individually are selling the Communist nations the rope with which to hang themselves must take into account the fact that many of the benefits of transfers are muted through the resistance or friction inherent in either transmission channels or the institutions of the recipient. To rephrase Lenin's metaphor, it is likely that a good deal of the "rope" is lost, misallocated, delayed, or otherwise damaged by the time it gets into the hands of the hangman. Moreover, effective utilization of the rope requires Communist states to make correspondingly large infrastructural investments that may, in fact, divert resources from direct military application.

Third, the impact of technology transfer cannot be assessed without some attention to the qualitative as well as quantitative dimensions of the process. On the one hand, successful technology transfer may depend heavily on the operation of some kind of critical mass phenomenon whereby both the amount and nature of what is imported become so great as to dwarf whatever institutional obstacles to diffusion and assimilation exist. On the other, as Frederic Fleron reminds us (1977: 59), successful usage depends not only on tools and machines but also on "the system of purposeful rational action" governing application and on "the system of cultural infrastructure necessary to support and in which to utilize" the technology provided by tools and machines. To these observations must be added Marshall Goldman's proposition (1976: 115) that a sale to the USSR does not necessarily mean that the Soviet economy will be able to adapt, innovate, or compete (like Japan) in the foreseeable future. "Linear improvements," he reminds us, are not the same as discontinuous advances in this area.

Interesting and important though these points may be, they provide us with few guidelines that can help illuminate the actual dimensions of technology transfer between Japan and the nations of the Communist world in an empirical fashion. For this reason, we will employ multiple indicators to help us measure the overall significance of the process. These include the following:

- quantitative and qualitative assessments of both the size and the content of Japanese trade relations with the USSR and PRC;
- quantitative measures of Japanese machinery exports to these nations (in line with the criteria for technology transfer laid out by Phillip Hanson, 1978 and others);

- analysis of Japan's high technology machine exports to the same recipients, as compared to these exports to Communist states by other Western nations (using the criteria developed by Kravalis et al., 1979, in the Office of East-West Policy and Planning, Industry and Trade Administration, U.S. Department of Commerce).

Unlike the blind men in the fable, we do not assume that the elephant we are trying to describe and analyze will be identical with any one of its disparate parts. In the absence of agreement on just what technology transfer involves, a multi-faceted approach seemed preferable to dogmatic insistence on a single kind of definition. Before proceeding to the study of technology transfer per se, however, it will be useful to examine first the larger context of Japanese trade relations with the Communist world.

The aggregate trade picture for Japan in 1977 shows that it maintained a healthy trade surplus with both European and Asian Communist nations: $1.04 billion for the former and $0.5 billion for the latter. Both figures are exclusive of invisible payments for shipping, tourism, and the like (MITI, 1978d: 243). In the case of trade with the USSR, such a surplus was repeated for each year between 1973 and 1978, with the official trade deficits of the earlier period (1956-1972, 1961 excepted) always being offset by the invisible payments mentioned above (Nisso Tu-o Bo'ekikai, 1978). The 1978 surplus is due to a 29.7 percent increase in exports to the USSR over 1977 levels, coupled with a mere 1.3 percent rise in imports. As a result, the 1978 trade surplus with the USSR stood at $1.06 billion, only slightly less than the all-time high of $1.08 billion registered in 1976. Indeed, Czechoslovakia is the only Communist nation with which Japan has run a small trade deficit, apparently owing to sizeable Japanese imports of Czech malt (for beer) and some machinery (MITI, 1978d: 248).

From an historical perspective, Japan's trade with the USSR has expanded at an extremely rapid rate in the three decades since World War II, as Table 1 demonstrates. Such trade increased under the impetus of a variety of factors: (1) the development by Japan of a more autonomous foreign policy strategy, dedicated to equidistance and multilateralism in foreign

**TABLE 1 Japanese-Soviet Trade, 1946-1978
(in thousands of dollars)**

Year	Exports		Imports		Total	
1946	24		0		24	
1947	140		2,004		2,144	
1948	4,385		2,670		7,055	
1949	7,360		1,933		9,293	
1950	723		738		1,461	
1951	0		28		28	
1952	150		459		609	
1953	7		2,101		2,108	
1954	39		2,249		2,288	
1955	2,710		3,070		5,780	
1956	760		2,860		3,620	
1957	9,294	(100)	12,324	(100)	21,618	(100)
1958	18,100	(195)	22,150	(180)	40,250	(186)
1959	23,026	(248)	39,490	(320)	62,516	(289)
1960	59,976	(645)	87,025	(706)	147,001	(680)
1961	65,380	(703)	145,409	(1,180)	210,789	(975)
1962	149,390	(1,607)	147,309	(1,195)	296,699	(1,372)
1963	158,136	(1,701)	161,940	(1,314)	320,076	(1,481)
1964	181,810	(1,956)	226,729	(1,840)	408,539	(1,890)
1965	168,358	(1,811)	240,198	(1,949)	408,556	(1,890)
1966	214,022	(2,308)	300,361	(2,437)	514,383	(2,379)
1967	157,688	(1,697)	453,918	(3,683)	611,606	(2,829)
1968	179,018	(1,926)	463,512	(3,761)	642,530	(2,972)
1969	268,247	(2,886)	461,563	(3,745)	729,810	(3,376)
1970	340,932	(3,668)	481,038	(3,093)	821,970	(3,802)
1971	377,267	(4,059)	495,880	(4,024)	873,147	(4,039)
1972	504,179	(5,425)	593,906	(4,819)	1,098,085	(5,079)
1973	484,210	(5,210)	1,077,701	(8,745)	1,561,911	(7,225)
1974	1,095,642	(11,789)	1,418,143	(11,507)	2,513,785	(11,628)
1975	1,626,200	(17,497)	1,169,618	(9,491)	2,795,818	(12,933)
1976	2,251,894	(24,230)	1,167,441	(9,473)	3,419,335	(15,817)
1977	1,933,877	(20,808)	1,421,875	(11,537)	3,355,752	(15,523)
1978	2,502,195	(26,923)	1,441,723	(11,698)	3,943,918	(18,244)

NOTE: The figures in parentheses indicate percentage increments after 1957.
SOURCE: Communication from Japanese-Soviet-East European Trade Association, Tokyo, Japan, 1979.

affairs; (2) the simultaneous eclipse of the old, bipolar structures of the international order; (3) sheer economic necessity (e.g., the demand for larger and larger amounts of raw materials and fuels to service the world's second largest industrial economy); and (4) increased Soviet receptivity to the idea of Far Eastern trade owing to the decision to open up Siberia for intensive economic development.

In recent years, the PRC has overtaken the USSR as Japan's major trading partner and export market among the Communist states. (See Table 2.) Between 1977 and 1978, Japanese exports to China increased by 47 percent and imports by 32 percent, as compared to 26 percent and 0.6 percent for trade with the USSR (MITI, 1978c: 68). Also, in a "best 20" list of Japan's trading partners, the PRC continued to outrank the USSR in 1978: in exports, the PRC was in eighth place (versus tenth for the USSR) and in imports, tenth place (versus thirteenth for the USSR) (MITI, 1978b: 144-145).

Japanese trade with Eastern Europe remains relatively small and stagnant. Comparisons to trade linkages with her giant Communist neighbors tell the story at a glance, as Table 3 indicates. Even in the case of Poland and Rumania, Japan's major Eastern European trading partners, trade increments in 1978 were either small (Poland, 1.1 percent) or on the negative side (Rumania, -16.6 percent).

In the time frame of the last decade, Japanese reliance on Communist states as either markets for exports or sources of imports has not been very great. For example, in an age when sources of energy promise to become the new yardstick of international dependency relationships, Japanese imports of mineral fuels from Communist sources fell by 8.2 percent between 1976 and 1977. Overall, Communist states and Western Europe combined appear insignificant as energy sources (4.4 percent) compared to the Middle East (64.1 percent), Asia (19.9 percent) and North America (6.5 percent) (MITI, 1978d: 141).

Table 4 provides a fuller picture. While Japanese trade with Communist states registered a 3.9 percent increase in exports and a 16.2 percent increase in imports, 1976-1977, export increments were far below those which Japan enjoyed with the developed nations (20.2 percent) or the Third World (21.7 percent) (Nippon, 1978: 70). Dependency on Communist sources increased rapidly only for imports, and even then the proportion of all Japanese imports remained quite small. Further, in almost every year since 1968, metals have formed the single most impor-

TABLE 2 Japanese-Chinese Trade, 1960-1978
(Compared with Japanese-Soviet Trade)
(in thousands of dollars)

Year	Exports	Imports	Total	As Percentage of Japanese-Soviet Trade
1960	2,726	20,724	23,455	16%
1961	16,639	30,895	47,534	23%
1962	38,460	46,020	84,480	28%
1963	62,417	74,599	137,016	43%
1964	152,739	157,750	310,489	76%
1965	245,036	224,705	469,741	115%
1966	315,150	306,237	621,387	108%
1967	288,294	269,439	557,733	91%
1968	325,438	224,185	549,624	86%
1969	390,803	234,540	625,343	86%
1970	568,878	253,813	822,691	100%
1971	578,188	323,172	901,360	103%
1972	608,920	491,116	1,100,036	100%
1973	1,039,493	974,010	2,013,503	129%
1974	1,984,475	1,304,768	3,289,243	131%
1975	2,258,577	1,531,076	3,789,653	136%
1976	1,662,568	1,370,915	3,033,483	89%
1977	1,938,643	1,547,344	3,485,987	104%
1978	3,048,748	2,030,292	5,079,040	129%

SOURCE: K. Ogawa, "Economic and Trade Relations Between Japan and the Soviet Union, China, and the Socialist Countries of Europe." (Unpublished monograph for the Japanese Association for Trade with the Soviet Union and the Socialist Countries of Europe. Tokyo, 1979), p. 35, and Table 1.

tant component of Japan's export dealings with Communist states (range: 39.8-46.9 percent), followed by machinery and equipment (range: 28.3-35.7 percent). (In the single exception, 1975, machinery exceeded metals by only 0.2 percentage points.)

Information regarding Japan's export ties and dependencies, by world region as well as by commodity sector, is provided in Table 5. The results confirm the conclusions drawn from previous tables. Japan's exports to the Communist world accounted for only about one-sixteenth of her total exports, and the proportion for each individual commodity sector ranges only from 0.3 percent to 14 percent. In technology-intensive areas such as machinery, Japanese sales amounted to but 3.1 percent of her total sales

TABLE 3   Japanese Trade with Eastern Europe, The USSR,
and the PRC (in thousands of dollars)

Year	Total with Eastern Europe	Eastern Europe as Percentage of Trade with USSR	Eastern Europe as Percentage of Trade with PRC
1970	217,848	26.5%	26.5%
1975	787,119	28.2%	20.8%
1976	745,249	21.8%	24.6%
1977	943,660	28.1%	27.1%
1978	927,834	23.5%	18.3%

SOURCE: K. Ogawa, "Economic and Trade Relations Between Japan and the Soviet Union, China, and the Socialist Countries of Europe." (Unpublished monograph for the Japanese Association for Trade with the Soviet Union and the Socialist Countries of Europe. Tokyo, 1979), p.32; and Tables 1 and 2.

TABLE 4   Japanese Trade with
Communist Nations 1968-1977

Year	Percentage of All Exports	Percentage of All Imports
1968	4.5%	6.5%
1973	5.3%	6.0%
1974	7.1%	5.1%
1975	8.4%	5.2%
1976	7.0%	4.4%
1977	6.1%	4.7%

SOURCE: Ministry of International Trade and Industry (MITI), White Paper on International Trade, Japan, 1978: Summary (Tokyo: MITI, 1978) pp. 240, 241.

abroad in this sector. Exports of metals and chemicals, which are usually not channels for technology transfer (unless plants and know-how are included), occupied first place and were aimed primarily at China, not the USSR or Eastern Europe.

To conclude our general overview of Japan's trade linkages with the Communist world, it is useful to construct a "best 20" list of Japan's trading partners and to note changes in rank orderings over the last decade. Information for this purpose is provided in Figure 1 and a graphic summary of the results in Figure 2. From these we see that while the USSR has risen

TABLE 5 Japanese Exports, Communist and Noncommunist World, 1977
(in millions of dollars)

		Developed Areas	United States	EEC	Oceania & South Africa	Developing Areas	Asia	Middle East	Communist Bloc	China	USSR	All Areas
Foodstuffs:	$ value	382	200	77	40	485	221	114	3	0.1	1	870
	% of total exports	43.9	23.0	8.9	4.6	55.9	25.4	13.1	0.3	0	0.1	—
Raw Materials and Fuel:	$ value	249	48	149	30	396	320	21	47	12	14	692
	% of total exports	36.0	6.9	21.5	4.3	57.2	46.2	3.0	6.8	1.7	2.0	—
Light Industrial Products:	$ value	4,322	2,095	1,002	614	5,096	2,774	1,531	687	240	289	10,106
	% of total exports	42.8	20.7	9.9	6.1	50.4	27.4	15.2	6.8	2.4	2.9	—
Textiles:	$ value	1,393	669	233	308	2,812	1,554	826	494	198	201	4,700
	% of total exports	29.6	14.2	5.0	6.6	59.8	33.1	17.6	10.5	4.2	4.3	—
Nonmetallic Mineral mfg.:a	$ value	559	337	89	74	544	248	234	43	2	26	1,146
	% of total exports	48.8	29.4	7.8	6.5	47.5	21.6	20.4	3.8	0.2	2.3	—
Heavy Industrial Products:	$ value	32,697	17,146	7,424	2,840	31,336	13,596	7,197	4,095	1,666	1,580	68,129
	% of total exports	48.0	25.2	10.9	4.2	46.0	20.0	10.6	6.0	2.4	2.3	—
Chemicals:	$ value	1,246	488	395	219	2,449	2,075	134	604	343	152	4,300
	% of total exports	29.0	11.3	9.2	5.1	57.0	48.3	3.1	14.0	8.0	3.5	—
Metal Products:	$ value	5,174	3,305	617	437	6,955	3,364	1,878	1,956	1,106	638	14,084
	% of total exports	36.7	23.5	4.4	3.1	49.4	23.9	13.3	13.9	7.9	4.5	—
Machinery and Equipment	$ value	26,276	13,353	6,412	2,184	21,932	8,156	5,185	1,536	217	790	49,744
	% of total exports	52.8	26.8	12.9	4.4	44.1	16.4	10.4	3.1	0.4	1.6	—
% of total exports by area:		47.2	24.0	11.0	4.0	46.7	21.0	11.0	6.0	2.0	2.0	100.0
Total $ value (millions):		$38,002	19,717	8,736	3,533	37,582	17,126	8,884	4,910	1,939	1,934	80,495

a. Cement, ceramics, tiles, flat glass and glass products, pearls.
SOURCE: Ministry of International Trade and Industry (MITI), White Paper on International Trade, Japan, 1978: Summary (Tokyo: MITI, 1978) Appendix, pp. 76-77.

FIGURE 1: Japan's Trading Partners: A "Best 20" Listing, 1969-1970

Rank	1969 Export	1969 Import	1972 Export	1972 Import	1975 Export	1975 Import	1976 Export	1976 Import	1977 Export	1977 Import
1	USA	USA	USA	USA	USA	USA	USA	USA	USA	USA
2	S. Korea	Australia	Canada	Australia	Liberia	S. Arabia	S. Korea	S. Arabia	S. Korea	S. Arabia
3	Hong Kong	Iran	Taiwan	Iran	P.R.C.	Iran	Liberia	Australia	W. Germany	Australia
4	Taiwan	Canada	Liberia	Indonesia	S. Korea	Australia	Australia	Iran	Taiwan	Indonesia
5	Liberia	Philippines	S. Korea	Canada	Iran	Indonesia	Taiwan	Indonesia	Liberia	Iran
6	Canada	USSR	U.K.	S. Arabia	Indonesia	Canada	USSR	Canada	S. Arabia	Canada
7	Philippines	W. Germany	W. Germany	W. Germany	Taiwan	Kuwait	W. Germany	U.A.E.	Australia	U.A.E.
8	Australia	S. Arabia	Hong Kong	USSR	Australia	U.A.E.	S. Arabia	Kuwait	Hong Kong	Kuwait
9	Thailand	Malaysia	Australia	Kuwait	W. Germany	P.R.C.	Hong Kong	S. Korea	U.K.	S. Korea
10	W. Germany	Indonesia	Singapore	U.K.	USSR	S. Korea	Iran	P.R.C.	P.R.C.	Malaysia
11	P.R.C.	U.K.	Indonesia	P.R.C.	Singapore	USSR	P.R.C.	Malaysia	USSR	P.R.C.
12	U.K.	India	P.R.C.	Philippines	U.K.	W. Germany	Indonesia	W. Germany	Iran	W. Germany
13	Singapore	Zambia	Thailand	S. Korea	Hong Kong	Philippines	Canada	Brunei	Indonesia	USSR
14	Okinawa	S. Africa	USSR	Taiwan	S. Arabia	Brunei	Singapore	Taiwan	Singapore	Taiwan
15	S. Africa	Kuwait	Philippines	S. Africa	Canada	Brazil	U.K.	USSR	Canada	U.K.
16	USSR	P.R.C.	Netherlands	India	Panama	S. Africa	Panama	Thailand	Thailand	Brazil
17	Indonesia	Trucial States	Panama	Malaysia	Philippines	Taiwan	Philippines	U.K.	Panama	Philippines
18	S. Vietnam	Mexico	Brazil	France	Thailand	U.K.	Netherlands	Brazil	Netherlands	S. Africa
19	Greece	Peru	Greece	Thailand	Brazil	Thailand	Thailand	India	Philippines	India
20	Netherlands	Chile	S. Africa	Brazil	S. Africa	Malaysia	France	Philippines	Greece	Thailand

SOURCE: Ministry of International Trade and Industry (MITI), Tsusho hakusho soron (Tokyo: MITI, 1970, pp. 414-415; 1973, pp. 420-421; 1976, pp. 476-477; 1977, pp. 10-11). Nippon, A Chartered Survey of Japan, 1978 (Tokyo: Kokusei-sha, 1978), pp. 77-78.

FIGURE 2: **Changing Status of Selected Japanese Trading Partners, 1969-1977**

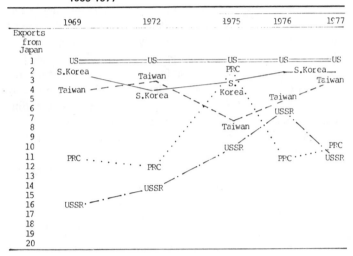

FIGURE 2 (CONTINUED)
CHANGING STATUS OF SELECTED JAPANESE TRADING PARTNERS, 1969-77

SOURCE: See Figure 1.

steadily in importance as an export market, the PRC—though less advanced and therefore less able to absorb Japanese technology—has almost always outranked the Soviet "elder brother." The picture changes little when we shift our attention to the import side. The USSR declines rather steadily in importance, while the PRC, after an initial rise in significance, seems to have settled into a holding pattern over the past few years. (Whether or not the implementation of the "four modernizations" so triumphantly proclaimed for the PRC in 1978-1979 will alter this picture, time alone will tell.) Top billing in both cases remains the preserve of the market economies: the United States, Australia and, to a great extent, Taiwan.

Interesting though such figures and tables may be, they still leave the picture regarding technology transfer in somewhat fuzzy focus. If we employ some qualitative assessments of the situation—and take Japanese-Soviet deals as a prototype—the opportunities for technology transfer still seem rather limited. While turnkey plants have been provided along with the simple sale of equipment, many of these have occurred in the areas of chemical and fertilizer production rather than for machinery production per se. It is debatable whether such transfers involve either high technology or that relevant to military applications. By the same token, a number of the machinery deals have covered construction and mining equipment. Neither of these necessarily contains leading-edge technology or is technology intensive. (Our judgments in both instances are based on the items *excluded* from the list of high technology exports as drawn up by the U.S. Department of Commerce [Kravalis et al., 1979: 44-55].)

In other channels such as licensing agreements, it is unclear just how many such arrangements are involved. One source which does not aggregate very precisely) maintains many, but provides few examples (Mathieson, 1979: 154-155, 158, 233-234; Hanson, 1978: 22-23). The figure of 200 agreements advanced is admittedly conjectural, and it still equals only 8.5 percent of all licensing arragements between Western nations and members of Comecon (China excluded). To date, the only cases of joint development projects involve the Sakhalin Continental Shelf Exploration Project with the USSR and a joint restaurant venture with China (Mathieson, 1979: 92-96).

A somewhat clearer picture of the dynamics of technology transfer between Japan and the Communist world emerges once we utilize machinery transfers (exports by Japan and imports by the USSR and/or the PRC) as a composite indicator. Table 6 illustrates Japanese machinery exports to the USSR as a proportion of all Japanese exports to the Soviet Union for 1967–1976. Several facts stand out, based on the table and related data. The first is Japan's ability to capture a sizeable portion of the Soviet import market at an early date, as compared to other Organization for Economic Cooperation and Development (OECD) nations (OECD, 1978: 73–74). Second, as a source of Soviet machine imports, the Japanese contribution remains relatively stable over time. In 1976, Japanese machines accounted for 13.9 percent of Soviet machinery imports, roughly the same as in 1965 (13.0 percent). (Interim fluctuations never exceeded three percentage points on either side of these figures.)

Third, as Table 6 shows, there was no steady upward or downward movement in Japanese machinery exports to the USSR as a share of total exports to the USSR, at least until 1977. This stands in contrast to the figures for U.S. and British machinery transfers to the USSR during the same period (OECD, 1978: 73–74). Despite the passage of a decade during which the trade relationship between the two nations might presumably have "matured," the relative significance of Soviet purchases to Japanese exporters rose little between 1967 and 1976. In 1977, however, Soviet purchases increased by about one-third over 1976, with an additional increment of 18 percent in 1978 to bring the total share of Japanese machinery exports (as a proportion of all exports) to the USSR to 47.3–47.8 percent (Ogawa, 1979: 33; Table 7).

But the fact remains that overall increases in Japanese machinery exports to the *entire* Communist bloc, 1976–1977, were still below increments to other world regions: 7.8 percent to Communist nations compared to 29 percent to North America, 27.4 percent to Asia, 36.4 percent to the Middle East, 29.8 percent to Latin America, and 10.1 percent to Africa. Using machinery exports as an indicator, we can therefore conclude that technology transfer to the Communist bloc from Japan as a share of technology transfer from Japan to the world at large remained fairly constant, 1973–1977, in the range of 2.8–5.6 percent.

TABLE 6   Japanese Machinery Exports to USSR
(As Percentage of All Japanese Exports to USSR)
1967-1976 (in thousands of dollars)

Year	Total Exports $ Value	Machinery Exports $ Value	Machinery Exports % of Total
1967	157,688	53,055	33.6%
1968	179,018	50,301	28.1%
1969	268,247	73,969	27.6%
1970	340,932	108,717	31.9%
1971	377,267	122,138	32.4%
1972	504,180	203,542	40.4%
1973	484,210	176,813	36.5%
1974	1,095,642	239,440	21.9%
1975	1,626,200	574,349	35.3%
1976	2,251,894	697,808	31.0%

SOURCE: Ministry of International Trade and Industry (MITI), Tsusho hakusho soron (Tokyo: MITI, 1970, pp. 667-668; 1973, pp. 735-736; 1976, pp. 907-909; 1977, pp. 845-846).

TABLE 7   Japanese Machinery Exports By Region
1978 (in thousands of dollars)

	Machinery Exports	All Exports	Machinery as % of Total
Total	$51,120,220	$79,467,933	64.3%
Industrialized Western Nations	27,144,870	37,268,971	72.8%
LDC	22,158,104	37,017,595	59.9%
Communist Bloc	1,817,140	5,181,217	35.1%
USSR	952,194	2,012,288	47.3%
PRC	460,546	2,311,332	19.9%
EE	310,269	554,815	55.9%

SOURCE: Ministry of International Trade and Industry (MITI), Summary Report, Trade of Japan, No. 10 (Tokyo: MITI, 1978), pp. 128-129.

(Increases between 1973 and 1975 were followed by decreases to 3.6 percent and 3.1 percent in 1978 and 1979 [Mathieson, 1979; 110].)

The picture for 1978 leads even further toward the conclusion that, viewed from the perspective of machinery exports, technology transfer to the Communist bloc from Japan may be a false issue. Table 7 demonstrates that machinery exports to the USSR, PRC, and East Europe are of less significance proportionately than those to the industrialized Western nations or the Third World, both in the dollar amounts involved and in their place in the overall commodity structure of Japanese exports. Compilation of a "best 20" list for Japanese machinery exports alone in 1978 reveals that as purchasers, the Soviet Union ranks only fifteenth and China twenty-fourth (MITI, 1978c: 138–139). (In each instance, these *sectorial* rankings are lower than the *general* rankings for either partner: eighth place for the PRC and tenth place for the USSR in 1978.) In 1978, the USSR accounted for but 0.8 percent of the dollar value of Japanese machinery sales abroad, and the PRC for even less, 0.02 percent (MITI, 1978c: 146–147).

The Chinese case merits some special attention apart from those general conclusions. During the late 1960s, Japanese machinery exports to the PRC diminished in importance, from 25 percent of all exports to that nation in 1965 to 10 percent in 1968. By 1971, the total had risen again to only 21 percent (JETRO, 1972: 85). Subsequent fluctuations appear almost random, despite China's retreat from the excesses of the Great Cultural Revolution. Machinery shipments accounted for 30.8 percent of exports to the PRC in 1975, 23.8 percent in 1976, 11.2 percent in 1977, and 20.9 percent in 1978 (Ogawa, 1979: 36). In contrast to the Soviet case, metals have consistently accounted for the largest share of Japanese exports to the PRC from 1965 to the present; chemicals have vied with machinery for second place since roughly 1970.

As we indicated at the outset of this chapter, however, machinery exports represent only one of several possible indicators of technology transfer—and probably one that is still too crude for purposes of developing recommendations for changing export controls, based on a cost-benefit calculation for the United States and its partners in the Western alliance. For this reason, the remainder of this chapter is devoted to an examination of Japanese technology transfer to the Communist bloc from two additional statistical perspectives. The first utilizes the definition of technology intensive products (as opposed to simply machinery) developed by Raymond Mathieson (1979: 4–11), an

TABLE 8 Soviet Imports of Technology-Intensive Products From Japan
1973 (in millions of rubles)

Classification	Description of Technology Imports	Total Imports	From Western Industrial Capitalist Countries	From Japan	Japan's Percentage of	
					All Imports	Imports from West
100	Machines and equipment for industrial and transport equipment	5,337.5	1,433.4	159.8	3.0	11.1
101-3	Metal-cutting machine tools	253.0	108.8	7.2	2.8	6.6
110+	Forging and pressing equipment	86.6	29.7	13.5	15.6	45.4
111	Power generating and electrical equipment	278.4	34.6	—*	—	—
112	Electrolytic industry anodes	3.6	3.6	3.6	100.0	100.0
113	Cable and wire	107.3	21.9	—	—	—
120	Mineral mining equipment	12.4	7.1	—	—	—
123	Metallurgical equipment	133.1	54.7	2.3	1.7	4.2
127	Oil-refining equipment	13.9	2.7	—	—	—
128	Oil and gas exploration and production equipment	31.7	4.4	—	—	—
130	Hoisting gear	278.3	26.1	6.5	2.3	24.9
140	Food industry equipment	160.7	38.3	1.4	0.9	3.6
142	Refrigeration and air-conditioning equipment	57.1	2.9	—	—	—
144	Textile industry equipment	121.9	28.6	3.3	2.7	11.5
150	Chemical industry equipment	430.7	240.7	61.9	14.4	25.7

TABLE 8   Soviet Imports of Technology-Intensive Products From Japan
1973 (in millions of rubles) (Cont)

Classification	Description of Technology Imports	Total Imports	From Western Industrial Capitalist Countries	From Japan	Japan's Percentage of	
					All Imports	Imports from West
151	Timber, pulp/paper and woodworking equipment	128.6	111.7	2.2	1.7	2.0
154	Excavation equipment	130.1	66.9	0.1	0.08	0.1
155	Compressor equipment	68.2	20.7	0.3	0.4	1.4
157	Printing industry equipment	43.3	16.3	1.9	4.4	11.6
159	Electronic industry equipment	34.6	10.1	5.4	15.6	53.5
170-1	Instruments and laboratory equipment	136.5	39.8	6.2	4.5	15.6
172	Medical instruments and equipment excluding chemopharmaceutical ind.	62.2	10.9	1.8	2.9	16.5
190	Rolling stock and auxiliary equipment	307.4	6.3	—	—	—
191	Freight lorries and garage equipment	402.0	0.4	—	—	—
192	Ships and marine equipment	454.5	96.2	6.3	1.4	6.5
	Total	3,736.1	983.4	123.9	N.O.S.	N.O.S.
	Machines and equipment N.O.S.	1,601.4	450.0	35.9	N.O.S.	N.O.S.

*Not applicable
N.O.S., not otherwise specified
SOURCE: Raymond Mathieson, Japan's Role in Soviet Economic Growth: Transfer of Technology Since 1965 (New York: Praeger Publishers, 1979), pp. 8-9.

economic geographer. The second applies the high technology list of the Department of Commerce mentioned earlier. The next tables and charts summarize our findings and, more importantly, complete the basic picture of the present state of affairs regarding technology transfer in preparation for projections and predictions about the future in Chapter III.

The first set of data relating specifically to technology transfer summarizes the relationship between Japan and the USSR in 1973, using Mathieson's definition. In that year, Japan appears as a critical supplier among all Western nations in only a few selected areas: metal cutting and machine tools, electrolytic industry anodes, hoisting gear, and equipment for the chemical and electronic industries. Among Soviet suppliers on a worldwide basis, Japan figured prominently in only three sectors: electrolytic industry anodes (100 percent), chemical industry equipment (14 percent), and electronic industry equipment (15 percent).

By 1977 the picture had altered somewhat (Table 9). Of all Western suppliers of technology intensive items, Japanese sources played a prominent role in the following areas: power generating and electrical equipment (40.6 percent), oil refining equipment (87 percent), chemical industry equipment (21 percent), excavation equipment (36 percent), and compressor equipment (19 percent). Only in the area of oil refining equipment (36 percent) did Japan occupy a leading place among Soviet suppliers on an international basis. Meanwhile, for some of the traditional leading areas circa 1973, Japan had already yielded its dominant position.

An assessment of Japan's importance to the USSR as a source of advanced technology must also take into account the cross-national picture. For this reason, Table 9 provides data on the role of the United States and the Federal Republic of Germany (FRG) in terms of technology intensive exports. According to Soviet import statistics, American sources were important in the following areas: oil and gas production and exploration equipment (33 percent of Western imports, 17 percent of world imports), excavation equipment (64 percent of Western imports, 21 percent of world imports), compressor equipment (42 percent of Western imports, 10 percent of world imports), and electronic industry equipment (39 percent of Western imports, 11 percent of all imports). In many instances, the United States appears a direct competitor of Japan. Thus, restrictions on the exports of

TABLE 9 Technology Transfer and Soviet Sources: A Comparison of Imports of Machinery and Equipment by Product and Region (Japan, United States, West Germany) 1977 (millions of rubles)

Classification & Description (Per Table 8)	Total Imports (A)	Imports from West (B)	Imports from Japan (C)	Japan's Percentage of		Western Percentage of Imports (B/A)
				All Imports (C/A)	Imports from West (C/B)	
101-3	626.7	262.7	21.1	3.7	8.0	41.9
110+	232.8	9.8	—*	0.0	0.0	4.2
111	416.2	27.1	11.0	2.6	40.6	6.5
112	n.a.a	33.8	6.3	n.a.	18.6	n.a.
113	177.5	9.0	—	0.0	0.0	5.1
120	36.3	11.8	—	0.0	0.0	32.5
123	450.0	—	—	0.0	0.0	0.0
127	70.7	29.3	25.5	36.1	87.0	41.4
128	126.3	64.3	—	0.0	0.0	50.9
130	630.7	1.2	—	0.0	0.0	0.2
140	240.5	62.0	.7	.3	1.1	25.8
142	46.0	2.4	—	0.0	0.0	5.2
144	298.5	69.2	4.2	1.4	6.1	23.2
150	1,722.3	1,362.2	286.1	16.6	21.0	79.1
151	250.5	49.7	6.3	2.5	12.7	19.8
154	149.0	48.0	17.3	11.6	36.0	32.2
155	162.7	40.5	7.7	4.7	19.0	24.9
157	54.2	21.7	2.4	4.4	11.1	40.0
15931, 15932, 15941	77.4	24.8	2.0	2.6	8.1	31.9
170 (171, 178, 179)	255.8	73.1	9.9	3.9	13.5	28.6
172	119.0	30.8	4.2	3.5	13.6	25.9
190	471.2	0.5	—	0.0	0.0	0.1
191	764.9	0.5	—	0.0	0.0	0.1
192	918.3	302.5	42.2	4.6	14.0	32.9
All machines & equip. (gen'l)	11,466.2	3,743.4	684.9	6.0	18.3	32.6

a. Not Available

* Not Applicable

SOURCE: Vneshnaia torgovlia SSSR v 1977 godu, Statisticheskii sbornik (Moscow: Statistika, 1978), Raymond Mathieson, Japan's Role in Soviet Economic Growth: Transfer of Technology Since 1965 (New York: Praeger Publishers, 1979), pp. 8-9.

TABLE 9 (Continued)

| | U.S. Percentage of | | | FRG Percentage | |
Imports from U.S. (D)	All Imports (D/A)	Imports from West (D/B)	Imports from FRG (E)	All Imports (E/A)	Imports from West (E/B)
1.3	0.2	0.5	126.7	20.2	48.2
—	0.0	0.0	7.8	3.4	79.6
—	0.0	0.0	6.1	1.5	22.5
—	0.0	0.0	—	0.0	0.0
.8	0.5	6.8	8.7	24.0	73.7
—	0.0	0.0	—	0.0	0.0
—	0.0	0.0	—	0.0	0.0
21.2	16.8	33.0	15.0	11.9	23.3
—	0.0	0.0	—	0.0	0.0
4.7	0.7	7.6	34.3	14.3	55.3
—	0.0	0.0	1.8	3.9	75.0
4.5	1.5	6.5	11.0	3.7	5.3
112.8	6.5	8.3	273.9	15.9	20.1
—	0.0	0.0	16.0	6.4	32.2
30.7	20.6	64.0	—	0.0	0.0
17.0	10.4	42.0	14.2	8.7	35.6
—	0.0	0.0	7.3	13.5	33.6
8.4	10.9	38.7	—	0.0	0.0
8.2	3.2	11.2	17.0	6.6	23.3
2.4	2.0	7.8	9.1	7.6	29.5
—	0.0	0.0	—	0.0	0.0
—	0.0	0.0	—	0.0	0.0
—	0.0	0.0	200.5	21.8	66.3
350.8	3.1	9.4	1,041.6	9.1	27.8

the former imposed through CoCom invariably affect the latter as well.

The "German connection" appears both complex and far reaching. The FRG functions as a major Western supplier for the USSR in a far greater number of areas than either the United States or Japan, if major means providing 33 percent or more of Soviet imports of a given item. Further, as an important international as well as a Western supplier, the FRG provides the USSR with 20 percent or more of her imports from all sources in forging and pressing equipment, equipment for mineral mining, and marine-related products (ships and equipment). Overall, the FRG provides 27.8 percent of Soviet imports of technology intensive items from Western sources and 9.1 percent on a worldwide basis (versus 9.4 percent and 3.1 percent from the United States, and 18.3 percent and 6.0 percent from Japan).

The raw data from Table 9 is translated into a comparative rank ordering of Soviet import sources by Table 10. In all of 24 cases, the FRG occupies first place, as opposed to five for the United States and three for Japan. The FRG provides over half of Western-based imports in at least five areas, versus one apiece for the United States and Japan.

Such findings attest to the fact that export controls designed to curb technology transfer from the West, when imposed through CoCom, probably affect U.S. allies proportionately more than the United States itself. In such a situation, claims of unfair advantage and discriminatory arm-twisting are likely to be heard with increasing frequency, unless (or except) when international crises render such restrictions acceptable. Conversely, controls which the United States accepts unilaterally can only work to her disadvantage in terms of their inability to effectively choke off the flow of technology to Communist nations.

In view of the ongoing debate over ways to measure technology transfer, it appears useful to add the high-technology definition of the Department of Commerce to the technology-intensive-products definition of Mathieson. Such a shift in definition does not significantly alter the conclusions already advanced regarding Japan's role as a source of technology for the Communist bloc. On an item by item basis, Japan accounts for roughly two-fifths or more of Soviet high technology imports in

44

TABLE 10   Comparison of Soviet Import Dependencies on the
West by Source (United States, Japan, West Germany)
1977

Classification and Description, Item Per Table 8	Rank Ordering		
	Japan (C/B)	United States (D/B)	W. Germany (E/B)
101-3	2	3	1
110+	n	n	*
111	1	n	2
112	1	n	n
113	n	n	n
120	n	2	*
123	n	n	n
127	*	n	n
128	n	1	2
130	n	n	n
140	3	2	*
142	n	n	*
144	2	1	3
150	2	3	1
151	2	n	1
154	2	*	n
155	3	1	2
157	2	n	1
15931, 15932, 15941	2	1	n
170, 171, 178, 179	2	3	1
172	2	3	1
190	n	n	n
191	n	n	n
192	2	n	*
All Machines and Equipment	2	3	1
Totals: First Rank	3	5	11
Second Rank	10	2	3
Third Rank	2	4	1
None	9	13	9
Over 50%	1	1	5

* = over 50%
n = none
SOURCE: Table 9.

TABLE 11   High Technology Items

Standard International Trade Classification	Description
71142	Jet and Gas Turbines for Aircraft
7117	Nuclear reactors
7142	Calculating machines (including electronic computers)
7143	Statistical machines (punch card or tape)
71492	Parts of office machinery (including computer parts)
7151	Machine tools for metal
71852	Glass-working machinery
7192	Pumps and centrifuges
71952	Machine tools for wood, plastic, etc.
71954	Parts and accessories for machine tools
71992	Cocks, valves, etc.
7249	Telecommunications equipment (excluding TV & radio receivers)
72911	Primary batteries and cells
7293	Tubes, transistors, photocells, etc.
72952	Electrical measuring and control instruments
7297	Electron and proton accelerators
7299	Electrical machinery, not otherwise specified (including electromagnets, traffic control equipment, signalling apparatus, etc.)
7341	Aircraft, heavier than air
73492	Aircraft parts
7351	Warships
73592	Special purpose vessels (including submersible vessels)
8611	Optical elements
8613	Optical instruments
86161	Image projectors (might include holograph projectors)
8619	Measuring and control instruments, not otherwise specified

SOURCE: U.S. Department of Commerce, "IW Exports to the USSR." Computerized tables. 1979.

TABLE 12 Selected CoCom Nations as Sources of Soviet High Technology Imports Comparative Importance by Item, 1972-1977

	Average Yearly Amounts (percentage)[a]					Rank Order of Importance				
	FRG	France	Japan	U.K.	U.S.	FRG	France	Japan	U.K.	U.S.
71142	45.1	5.4	0	10.4	0	1	3	n[b]	2	n
7117	16.0	0	0	0	0	1	n	n	n	n
7142	4.7	1.7	53.4	0.5	9.4	3	4	1	5	2
7143	21.9	29.3	6.4	18.6	13.5	2	1	5	3	4
71492	15.9	13.5	4.1	28.5	26.0	3	4	5	1	2
7151	45.7	6.0	9.2	3.8	10.2	1	4	3	5	2
71852	18.2	16.4	16.7	3.5	25.2	2	4	3	5	1
71952	75.7	1.4	0.5	0.2	0.6	1	2	4	5	3
71954	31.2	20.1	11.7	3.9	12.4	1	2	4	5	3
71992	14.8	27.9	18.6	1.1	1.4	3	1	2	5	4
7249	21.3	0	0	0	0	1	n	n	n	n
72911	5.7	44.0	21.6	16.8	10.9	5	1	2	3	4
7293	13.7	53.2	14.4	2.6	3.4	3	1	2	5	4
72952	23.5	17.1	8.9	11.9	14.6	1	2	5	4	3
7297	18.2	15.1	0	0	28.2	2	3	n	n	1
7299	40.2	10.5	11.1	5.5	11.3	1	4	3	5	2

TABLE 12 Selected Cocom Nations as Sources of Soviet High Technology Imports Comparative Importance by Item, 1972-1977 (Cont)

| | Average Yearly Amounts (percentage)[a] | | | | | Rank Order of Importance | | | | |
	FRG	France	Japan	U.K.	U.S.	FRG	France	Japan	U.K.	U.S.
7341	20.0	0	0	0	17.3	1	c	c	c	2
73492	15.6	0.4	0	61.1	10.4	2	4	c	1	3
7351c	—	—	—	—	—	—	—	—	—	—
73592	13.7	4.0	39.4	0	0	2	3	1	c	c
8611	45.6	7.4	20.0	4.0	8.3	1	4	2	5	3
8613	35.3	2.7	38.9	9.2	1.5	2	4	1	3	5
86161	62.7	0.8	9.2	4.6	4.9	1	5	2	4	3
8619	20.5	2.7	9.3	60.2	4.3	2	5	3	1	4

a. Calculated on the basis of share rather than dollar amount.
b. None
c. No data available
SOURCE: U.S. Department of Commerce, "IW Exports to the USSR." Computerized tables. 1979.

only three cases, as opposed to six for the FRG, two for France, two for Britain, and none for the United States. Japanese sources provide a third of high technology imports in no cases at all (FRG, two; France, two; Britain, one; United States, one); a fifth to a quarter in two cases (FRG, seven; France, two; Britain, one; United States, two); and less than one-tenth for eight items (FRG, two; France, ten; United States, eight; Britain, twelve). For six of the items included, Japan and France provide no sources at all. For the United States and Britain, this is true in fewer (four) cases, while it does not hold true in any instance for the FRG.

In a rank ordering of suppliers of high technology to the USSR among selected Western states, 1972–1977, Japan occurs first place for three commodities (FRG, eleven; France, five; Britain, three; United States, two). It comes in second in another five cases (FRG, seven; France, three; United States, six; Britain, one). Once again, such data implies that any effort by the United States to increase the stringency of CoCom controls will generally appear to allies as leading from weakness rather than strength. Insofar as such restrictions would be felt more strongly by other Western nations than by the United States, a favorable political reaction to such proposals by either Japan, the FRG, or Britain will hardly be forthcoming—at least not without some offer of trade-offs in other areas. In this conjunction it is worth noting that whereas in 1972 Japan ranked second and the United States sixth among the industrialized Western nations' sources of high technology transfers to the USSR, by 1976 Japan held her position by only a slim margin. The Japanese share of these transfers remained almost stable throughout the detente era, but the United States share as a proportion of the total almost doubled (Kravalis et al., 1979: 41).

III. THE FUTURE OF TECHNOLOGY TRANSFER BETWEEN JAPAN AND THE COMMUNIST NATIONS

T he past may or may not be prologue. Despite the relatively insignificant place that machinery and high technology items have occupied in Japanese trade with the PRC the picture may well change dramatically in the near future. Both sides, in February 1978, negotiated a $20 billion, two-way trade package for 1978-1985, in addition to the existing trade; In March 1979 both agreed to extend this Long-Term Trade Agreement to 1990, with a target of $40-60 billion. The package calls for Chinese exports to Japan of $10 billion worth of oil and coal, in exchange for $7-8 billion worth of Japanese plants and technology and $2-3 billion worth of machinery and construction materials (U.S. Department of Commerce, 1979a: 11). By 1979, Japan's plant exporters had signed 22 sales contracts worth $2.6 billion with the Chinese. Recent reports suggest that these deals will in fact be consummated—and at higher prices (Economist, 1979b).

Along the same lines, the Japan Economic Research Center (JERC), while cautioning Japanese manufacturers of finished consumer goods against undue optimism regarding the Chinese market, has underscored a very significant point in projecting the future of technology transfer between Japan and the PRC. The JERC contends that Chinese economic development is likely to approximate Japanese development, meaning reliance on highly motivated (and relatively lowly paid) labor, a high degree of capital formation—and a high level of technology imports, to extend the analogy of the Japanese experience (Silk, 1979). For these reasons, as well as others, China is likely to become even more important as a market for Japanese technology.

Predictions about Japanese-Soviet trade relations are more difficult, in part because of the recent disruptions occasioned by international crises. It is worth remembering, however, that Japanese machinery as a proportion of all exports to the USSR rose from less than one-third in 1976 to almost one-half in 1978, as the preceding Chapter showed. In addition, the 1978 figures for Japanese machinery exports by region, as cited in Table 7, may well alter dramatically under the combined impact of import restrictions by Western nations, the inability of the energy-poor LDCs to continue their industrialization drive (or the unwillingness of energy-rich Middle Eastern nations to accept the social and political consequences of such a drive), and the increasing importance of China as a machinery importer within the Communist bloc. In any event, efforts to forestall the technological advancement of nonmarket economies on the grounds of "national security" may contribute less to the U.S. national interest than would efforts to avoid undue strains on the economic and political fabric of the Western alliance. It is within this context that the analysis shifts to a consideration of the place that technology export occupies in Japanese foreign economic policy and foreign relations more generally. Such an approach further broadens the base on which to provide recommendations for U.S. export control strategies for the future.

On a global scale, technology transfer promises to be increasingly important in Japan's overall export strategies, as Figure 3 indicates. By 1974, the ratio of receipts to payments in technology trade had risen to .16 and by 1975 to .23, due chiefly to a growing trade in technology with the Communist bloc (Outline, 1977: 9). Japan, however, still lags behind other Western nations in her technology transfer ratio: United States, 10.0; Britain and France, 1.0; FRG, .40. In some cases, Japanese technology exports have been the end products of imports into Japan. Japanese companies have proven adept at obtaining basic process techniques from the United States or Western Europe, improving on them, and reexporting them to the Communist

FIGURE 3:   Japanese Technology Trade: Export-Import Ratios

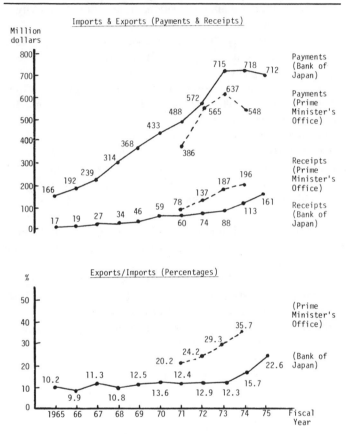

NOTES: 1. Bank of Japan figures are from the bank's "Balance of Payments Monthly," and the prime minister's office figures are from the office's report on the Survey of Research and Development in Japan.

2. The figures for fiscal 1975 are preliminary figures.

SOURCE: Outline of the White Paper on Science and Technology (Tokyo: Foreign Press Center, 1977), p. 12.

bloc. In 1968, Toyo Engineering obtained basic patents for an ammonia production process. The firm's alterations managed to increase output of this process by some 30 percent in a year's time. Mitsui and Co. then sold the process to the Soviet Union

(JETRO, 1977: 17–19). Interestingly enough, there seems little to indicate that Communist nations have a similar capacity to reexport processes rather than products.

Plant exports constitute the lion's share of technology transfer by Japan, with license and patent exports playing a minor role. In 1976, Japan's plant exports to the world totaled $6.5 billion, with a minimum value of $500 thousand per contract. (These figures put the $2 billion agreement for plant exports negotiated with the Chinese in 1978 into proper perspective.) The 1976 figure marks an increase of about one-third in the dollar value of plant exports over the previous year, even as total exports (calculated on a customs clearance basis) grew by only one-fifth.

The growing importance of plant exports in Japanese foreign trade, their shifting allocation by market region, and the distribution of exports by type of plant involved for the 1974–1976 period are described in Figures 4, 5, and 6. In terms of the kinds of plant exports involved, the transfer of chemical plants dominated the scene (39.3 percent of the total). These also registered the largest increments from 1975 to 1976. Orders worth over $100 million in this category included a LNG plant for the USSR. Plants to manufacture heavy electrical equipment also figured prominently. Overall, the importance of plant exports is demonstrated by the fact that 1976 levels registered an increase of 184 percent over 1974.

In regional markets, the Communist bloc was the primary customer for plant exports in 1976, purchasing almost 30 percent of the total involved. Although data for 1977–1979 is not yet available, subsequent purchases are likely to have been quite large because both the Soviet Union and Eastern Europe rank high in the lists of "major contracts won" (but not yet delivered) and "major enquiries outstanding" as of 1976 (JETRO, 1977: 2, 22–23). The Middle East occupied second place and Latin America third.

Two other features of Japan's plant exports merit our attention. One is their growing scale: the average value of such exports rose from $4.5 million in 1970 to $10.4 million in 1976 (without controls for price inflation). The increase was due in part to the increasing scale of the plants involved and because a larger

FIGURE 4:   Growing Importance of Plant Exports

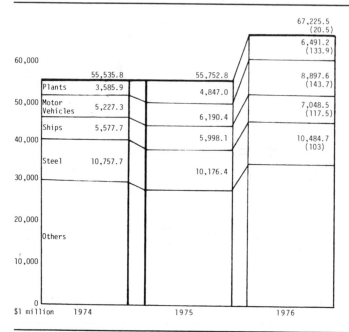

NOTES: 1.   Figures on plants are on an export licence basis, and those on others are on a customs clearance basis.
   2.   Figures in brackets denote the growth percentage over the previous year.
   Compiled from statistics of MITI and Ministry of Finance.
SOURCE: Japanese External Trade Organization (JETRO), Japan's Plant Exports, No. 11 (Tokyo: JETRO, 1977), p. 6.

number of turnkey projects involving installation, engineering, and training costs also appeared on the lists (JETRO, 1977: 4-5). Second, while plant exports play a growing role in Japan's foreign trade (8 percent by 1976), on a comparative basis they are still less important than in the case of the United States (25.5 percent), FRG (22.8 percent), and Britain (9.4 percent) (JETRO, 1977: 7). Supplier's credit (deferred installment payment) finances 73 percent of Japan's plant exports, even though buyer's credits (bank loans) are favored by the Communist states.

54

FIGURE 5: Japan's Plant Exports by Market Region

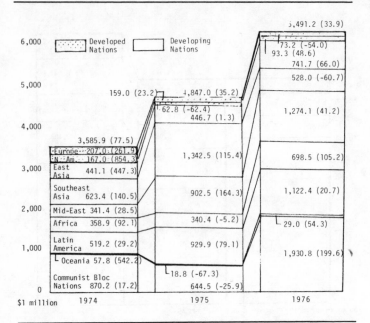

NOTES: 1. Figures in brackets denote the growth percentage over the previous year.
        2. "East Asia" are Republic of Korea, Taiwan, and Hong Kong.
           MITI, Plant Export Licence Statistics.
SOURCE: Japanese External Trade Organization (JETRO), Japan's Plant Exports, No. 11 (Tokyo: JETRO, 1977), p. 4.

Against this backdrop, it appears that the export of technology to willing and eager buyers—among them the Communist states—will remain an integral feature of Japanese economic growth strategy for the foreseeable future. Part of the explanation lies in what we would term the comparative structural advantage of the Japanese trading establishment. Given the preference of Communist nations for bilateral deals involving counterpurchase, barter, or buy-back arrangements, the Japanese *sogo shosha* have "a natural affinity for compensation-type negotiations" unmatched by their American, British, or German counterparts. This stems from a long history of multifaceted, multi-

FIGURE 6: Japan's Plant Exports by Plant Type

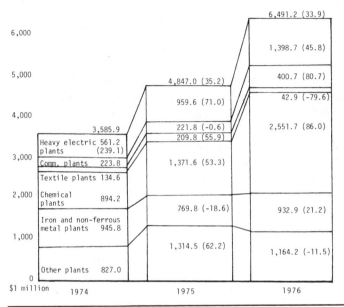

NOTES: 1. Above figures are on an export licence basis and concern plant exports worth $500,000 or more per case. Transportation machinery (ships, motor vehicles, rolling stock, etc.) is excluded.

2. The category "chemical plants" includes oil refineries, petrochemical plants, chemical fertiliser plants, pharmaceutical plants, synthetic fibre plants, paper/pulp plants, and cement plants.

3. The "other plants" include food and drink plants, resources-development/mining, harbours, steel structures, etc.

4. Figures in brackets denote the growth percentage over the previous year.

Compiled from Plant Export Licence Statistics of MITI

SOURCE: Japanese External Trade Organization (JETRO), Japan's Plant Exports, No. 11 (Tokyo: JETRO, 1977), p. 3.

lateral types of business and trading arrangements (Mathieson, 1979: 29, 236–237). In particular, the trading companies possess worldwide marketing networks, the financial ability to engage in triangular or "switch" trading—whereby Japanese firms sell the ruble credits they have earned to a third country or company at a markup—and an ability to dispose of a wide variety of unrelated products. The Japanese trading companies have also shown themselves adept in adjusting to the demands of East-West trade in a structural sense. In recent times, major traders have modified their organizational frameworks—especially where the sales function was geared primarily to handle a single item—in order to better manage the kinds of multidimensional projects that East-West trade involves (JETRO, 1977: 13-14).

There are, in addition, certain more deep-seated reasons for a continuing Japanese drive to export technology that must be understood in order to predict accurately future Japanese economic relations with the Communist bloc. The first of these, as Ohkawa and Rosovsky point out, is that exporting has been less a choice than a logical consequence of Japanese patterns of economic development in modern times. The reasons for Japanese export growth lie on the supply side of the equation—prices, quality of goods, product differentiations, and financing arrangements. Since the turn of the century, Japanese industry has not walked on "one leg" (cheap labor), as Americans would commonly like to believe, but on two (cheap labor *plus* a large infusion of imported technology). Together, these have yielded remarkable productivity increases (Ohkawa et al., 1973: 173–174, 177, 180–181). Since the beginning of the 1960s, shifts in traditional Japanese markets and export lines have been stimulated by new competition from other sources, e.g., the rest of East and Southeast Asia. For certain export items such as ceramics and textiles, this competition has spurred the Japanese on to seek new markets for new products—such as machinery, technology-intensive goods, and metals. The Communist states have proven willing purchasers.

Such considerations must weigh in any U.S. decision to adopt a policy that might curb Japanese technology exports, especially insofar as this move would require not just the reversal of one or two Japanese trading policies but a retreat from Japanese economic growth strategy in a larger sense (see Calleo and Rowland, 1973: 214). The political costs of any policy that visibly affects the growth rates of an ally would be enormous, to put it mildly. Precise information on how such costs appear to the Japanese is not easy to come by. We do know, however, that as of February 1979, Japanese public opinion favored voluntary restraints on exports to the United States and West Europe by only a small margin, 12 percent (USICA, 1979a: 2, citing *Gekkan Yoron Chosa*). Thus, it is hardly likely to welcome American-inspired efforts to get Japanese manufacturers to restrict their trade with Communist and Western states simultaneously, no matter how insignificant in quantitative terms this trade may be.

A second reason for regarding Japanese technology exports as an inalienable part of the Japanese political economy lies in the blueprint that Japanese economists have drawn up to guide their nation's economic future. According to the long-term economic forecasts developed by both the JERC ("The Future of the World Economy and Japan," 1975) and MITI ("A Long Term Vision for Industrial Structure," 1974), the composition of Japanese exports, from 1975 to 1985, is projected to change in ways that relate directly to the growth of East-West trade and technology transfer (Kojima, 1977: 130–136):

- machinery exports, especially products related to new technology and commodities incorporating electronics, will increase (by 22 percent according to JERC) (Kojima, 1977: 131);
- exports of plant construction material will increase;
- exports of chemicals, petrochemical products, plastics, iron, and steel will decline;
- the share of value-added, knowledge-intensive products in the chemical industry's output will rise;
- the export of precision instruments will increase (by 15.7 percent, JERC);
- regional increments will vary widely: from 11.0 percent to 11.1 percent for China; from 11.9 percent to 13.4 percent for Africa; from 20.6 percent to 22.4 percent for Oceania; and from 15.0 percent to 18.0 percent for the United States (Kojima, 1977: 135).

Along these same lines, JERC statistics indicate that in two areas—general machinery and sophisticated machinery—Japanese export ratios will continue to improve. In the first case, the proportion of the total products exported should increase from 7.9 percent in 1970 to 16.3 percent in 1985. More dramatic improvements are predicted for the export ratios of sophisticated machinery: from 22.1 percent in 1970 to 35.3 percent in 1974, 37.6 percent in 1980, and 39.8 percent in 1985 (Crawford and Okita, eds., 1978: 129–131). In broad perspective, the share of machinery in Japan's exports will rise from 50.2 percent in 1975 to 64.6 percent in 1985—and some of this must find its way to the Communist bloc. One indicator of the future importance of technology exports can be found in the Japanese plan to lead the world in integrated circuit components—and hence in the technology of computers and telecommunications—by the end of the century despite strong American competition. (By the end of 1979, the Japanese had already captured more than 40 percent of the U.S. market for advanced memory chips [New York Times, 1979].) Such shifts are a logical concommitant of the move away from labor-intensive, low productivity industries towards knowledge-intensive industries dependent on high value added per unit of raw material and worker. Labor intensive goods will be imported, chiefly from the LDCs (Crawford and Okita, eds., 1978: 125, 126).

Other factors as well will probably stimulate the search to expand trade with the Communist bloc. Not the least of these is Japan's well publicized raw materials dependency. This is particularly evident in the energy sector. Coal, which provided roughly one-sixth of Japan's energy needs in 1972, is almost two-thirds imported (Crawford and Okita, eds., 1978: 218). From this perspective, lower costs, transportation savings, and the guarantee of long-term, stable supplies through imports from either the USSR or the PRC will continue to make such nations attractive as trading partners.

The same holds true of oil imports, though here the long-term ties between Japan and either the USSR and the PRC are more difficult to predict. In the now-moribund Tyumen oil development project, the USSR promised Japan a maximum of 25 million tons of oil a year at a cost of $1 billion, with delivery scheduled to commence in 1980. Soviet behavior, however, indicated that any such deal would be fraught with political and strategic difficulties—as when, in March 1974, the Soviet side suddenly shifted its request for aid in constructing a Tyumen-Nakhodka pipeline to a proposal for Japanese assistance in building the BAM (a second Trans-Siberian railroad) so as to transport the oil by train (Curtis, 1977: 157-158). The failure of the Tyumen project to materialize means that the USSR still has not become a major supplier of petroleum products to Japan. Purchases from the Soviet Union were only 0.21 percent of Japanese crude oil imports in 1971, 0.49 percent in 1973, 0.03 percent in 1975, and 0.06 percent in 1976 (Japan National Committee, 1978: 18).

The Chinese, meanwhile, have persisted in their offers of oil without strings, even before the 1978 trade deal. But shipments to Japan remain small—and reserves underdeveloped—by comparison with the Soviet proposal: 1 million tons in 1973, 4.9 million tons in 1974, and about 8 million tons in 1975. (For 1982, 15 million tons are projected; further projections are questionable.) The Chinese feel that "oil for the lamps of Japan"—and for Japanese factories—can serve their political as well as economic advantage. Among other things, it mutes any Japanese enthusiasm for an energy alliance with the USSR. Thus, oil exports from the PRC to Japan have risen steadily even when Chinese exports in other areas have fallen. Worldwide inflation in oil prices notwithstanding, China's 1975 price-per-barrel quoted to Japan was 70 cents lower than in the previous year (Curtis, 1977: 169-170). The fact remains, however, that Chinese oil is heavy, with a high wax and sulfur content. It is therefore difficult and expensive to refine, especially by comparison with lighter crude from the USSR.

The effectiveness of this "energy bait" in stimulating Japanese exports to either the USSR or China remains difficult to assess, largely owing to the considerable uncertainty that still surrounds both the energy needs of the Communist states and their ability to bring new resources on stream quickly and economically (Economist, 1979f). In any case, additional energy sources, however small, do figure importantly in Japan's chosen strategy of resource diversification. As the world's second largest consumer of petroleum and as the single largest importer of crude oil, this strategy is dictated more by necessity than choice. By the mid-1970s, Japanese purchases accounted for 16.7 percent of the international oil market, in contrast to 13.4 percent for the United States, 13 percent for Britain, and 38 percent for the FRG, France, and Italy combined. By 1980, Japanese oil usage will amount to about 15 percent of the world's total (Curtis, 1977: 149).

Further, a major qualitative advantage to Japan in importing Communist oil is that it frees her somewhat from dependency on the "umbrella of the majors" (a phrase Japanese use to describe their overwhelming subordination to international oil consortia over which the Japanese have no control). Dependency in this case means that 72 percent of Japan's oil imports, 43 percent of her refining operations, and 47 percent of her distribution network is in the hands of the largest oil companies. Understandably, the Japanese would like nothing better than to spread the risk inherent in a possible disruption in their sources of supply (e.g., the 1973 oil embargo and the 1979 Iranian crisis), while freeing themselves from the complex interplay between OPEC, the oil companies, and Western nations regarding oil prices. To do this, they pursue trade linkages of all sorts wherever energy supplies exist.

The preceding analysis underscores the compelling economic considerations that push Japan to maintain and even increase her trade with the Communist bloc. In September 1979, the Japanese reaffirmed their willingness to keep up the flow of machinery and credit to the Soviet Union in return for timber, coal, and (potentially) oil from Siberia. The Japan National Oil Corporation has already committed some $100 million to an oil exploration project in the Sea of Okhotsk and recently agreed to another $70 million investment in the project. Japan has spent some $450 million to develop reserves of coking coal in Yakutsk in return for deliveries of 5 million tons annually over 20 years, starting in 1983, and the Japanese government seems receptive to Soviet requests for another $40 million in credits for this project. It should, however, be noted that there exists real Japanese resistance to Soviet blandishments in those areas in which there is a raw materials glut—paper pulp, asbestos, copper—or where Soviet preferences for buy-back arrangements promise to aggravate existing Japanese problems with production overcapacity (i.e., steel) (Economist, 1979d).

On the Chinese front, in December 1979 Japan offered the PRC its first governmental aid package of $1.5 billion, in return for Chinese exports of coal. Delays were occasioned not by debate within Japan over the political or military ramifications of Chinese technology imports but rather by the PRC's own retreat from its ambitious growth targets for 1979–1985. There was also internal resistance grounded in the Ministry of Finance's preference to lend as little as possible and by the Ministry of Foreign Affairs' concern that other nations in Southeast Asia (but not necessarily the USSR!) would believe the Chinese were feasting off what had been their own exclusive plate. (In the end, however, MITI got its way with arguments that loans for Chinese projects would yield more and cheaper raw materials for Japanese industry [Economist, 1979a and 1979e].)

Such trends confirm the observation of Japan's economists that its unique economic position and lack of raw materials render it dangerous for the nation to rely solely on commercial transactions to guarantee supplies to the economy. Diversification requires that the Japanese government take a large part of the responsibility as well as risk upon itself. Money and technology will continue to be exchanged for secure linkages with suppliers (Kosaka, 1977: 220).

At the same time, Japan's trading situation may move her to increase rather than decrease her trade connections with the Communist world. Traditionally she has generated trade surpluses not just because of her ability to sell manufactured goods to her raw materials suppliers—who, by definition, usually have poorly developed home markets—but rather because of her exports to the industrial world. More recently, even as the United States and European Economic Community (EEC) nations have been chipping away at Japan's nontariff barriers to their imports, Japan herself has shifted increasingly to direct competition with these technology-exporting countries in the area of high technology—semiconductors, numerically controlled machine tools, and computers. These industries have the largest planned increases in capacity during the Japanese investment cycle that began in 1978 (Economist, 1979c). Therefore, it appears that to the extent to which Japan's Western trading partners successfully push for orderly marketing arrangements, Japan will find herself thrown back upon an export substitution strategy. In this situation, Communist states would replace capitalist ones as the source of the international trade surplus Japan requires to pay for her raw materials imports. The state trading companies of the bloc nations, however, manifest less interest in Japanese manufactured goods than in her machines, technology, and know-how, given their own faltering rates of economic growth. Over time, such substitutions will increase the rate of Japanese technology transfer to the Communist world. It is not clear, as we shall see below, that general foreign policy or national security considerations can serve as effective constraints in the face of such economic pressures.

In the area of foreign policy, the idea of linkage as an effective foreign policy strategy does not seem to exert much of a hold on the thinking of representatives of Japanese business and governmental circles. The reasons for this are diverse. First, Japanese negotiating styles traditionally do not leave much room for the kind of flexible, well-developed, fallback strategies and sense of independent leverage that a policy of linkage, to be made effective, must have on at least one side (Blaker, 1977). Second, as Hiroshi Kimura, a political scientist at the Slavic Research Center of Hokkaido University, has demonstrated in a study of Japanese-Soviet fishing negotiations, there are certain cultural asymmetries between Japan and the USSR that make a linkage approach highly unlikely in their conduct of international relations. In particular, the Japanese penchant for seeing themselves as the weaker of the two parties in any conflict situation (as manifested in the psychology of *amae* or "dependence on the leniency of others") effectively rules out any projection of those images of strength and determination needed to make a linkage approach credible to the other side. To this consideration must be added both Japanese suspicion of "tactics" in their negative, Machiavellian connotation (as risky, dangerous, and ultimately self-defeating) and a penchant for proceeding according to reactive rather than "initiatory" patterns (Kimura, 1979). Third, Japanese attempts to exercise linkage have invariably faltered owing to its obvious military vulnerability, the absence of a large quantity of diversified resources with which to bargain, and because in many areas (e.g., the fisheries negotiations with the USSR), Japan's adversary has held the advantage. Roger Swearingen (1978: 172–184) reminds us that Japanese efforts to link a fisheries agreement to a political settlement vis-à-vis the Northern Territories has produced only a record of steady losses for the Japanese side. The 1956 Soviet-Japanese Fisheries Convention altered the status quo to the Soviet advantage without any substantive political gains for Japan. The pattern was repeated in the 1975 Limited Fisheries Accord as well as the 1977 agreement (which reduced the Japanese fishing quota from the 1.4 million ton limit of 1975 to 700 thousand tons from 1977 onward).

The Japanese experience with linkage in relations with other Communist nations has resulted in a similar lack of success. In the late 1960s, it was the PRC, not Japan, that successfully pursued Mao's version of a linkage strategy, as Figure 7 reveals. "Friendship trade" meant that the PRC traded chiefly with those companies that accepted either Zhou En-lai's "three political principles" (1958), the "trade principles" of 1960, or the "four conditions" of April 1970. As the figure indicates, this variant of Japanese-Chinese trade climbed steadily in dollar value over roughly a decade, despite Japanese political resistance. Conversely, "memorandum trade," which had a semiofficial basis, was endorsed by Japan's ruling Liberal Democratic Party, had the fiscal support of the Japanese Export-Import Bank, and declined steadily in importance during the same period (Lee, 1976: 141–169).

A similar pattern surfaces when we review Japanese trade relations with North Vietnam. Japanese threats to cut off foreign aid and trade after that country invaded Kampuchea (Cambodia) had no noticeable effect on the Vietnamese advance and consolidation of power. Roughly a year after the invasion, Japanese

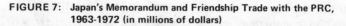

FIGURE 7: Japan's Memorandum and Friendship Trade with the PRC, 1963-1972 (in millions of dollars)

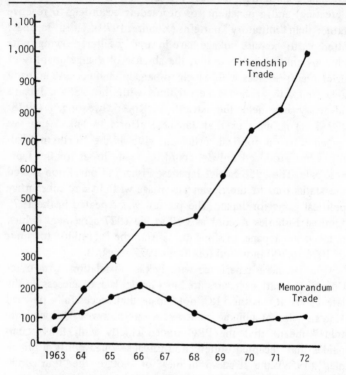

SOURCE: Chae Jin Lee, **Japan Faces China: Political and Economic Relations in the Post-War Era** (Baltimore: Johns Hopkins Press, 1976), p. 160.

officials were justifying their position by arguing that trade had to be preserved in order to safeguard their "lever"—despite the fact that their brief effort to make the mechanism operative had failed dismally.

Such experiences have undoubtedly dissuaded the Japanese foreign policy elite from trying to control technology transfer on political or general foreign policy grounds. Indeed, in a series of notes to Japanese trade negotiators in Tokyo in September 1979, the Ministry of Foreign Affairs indicated that it believed U.S. exports were severely hobbled by U.S. government policies linking American trade to human rights, pollution controls, and general political considerations (Economist, 1979c). Japanese scholars and officials alike argue that the Japanese should take the initiative to increase Soviet trust in Japanese intentions. To this they add that political issues (such as the return of the Northern Territories) should be subordinated to pragmatic economic calculations and that the overwhelming military might of the USSR renders linkage an impractical ploy (see, for example, Tokuoda, 1979). In general, the linkage concept also appears incompatible with the Japanese foreign policy strategy of "being friends with everybody." In terms of the Sino-Soviet conflict, this translates into a policy of evenhandedness. This policy follows from what one Japanese economist describes—using fencing terminology—as "being defenceless on all sides" (Crawford and Okita, eds., 1978: 226-227). Such considerations were reflected in a 1974 MITI White Paper that called on Japan to pursue a policy of "orderly imports" and "diversification of import markets" in order to insure stable supplies of essential resources. This meant that Japan had to "deepen her interchanges" with the Communist bloc as well as with Latin America and Africa (Crawford and Okita, eds., 1978: 170-171).[2]

Any assertion that the Japanese do not subscribe to linkage arguments and will not do so for the foreseeable future must be qualified on two fronts. First, the Japanese have not proven totally immune to the temptation to up the ante on the basis of a "China card." Despite Prime Minister Ohira's assurances to the Soviet Union following his December 1979 visit to Beijing, the fact remains that the $1.5 billion in loans pledged for construction projects in China will undoubtedly increase her ability to resist the USSR militarily, with better railroad and port facilities. The visit, while ostensibly dealing only with trade issues, also underlined the mutual interest of Japan and the PRC in defusing tensions on the Korean peninsula—and was seen by Japanese officials as confirming China's intention not to permit an effective North Korean military threat aimed southwards. The Japanese have also taken a calculated political risk vis-à-vis the USSR in their commitment to help the PRC exploit oil and gas resources in the Gulf of Bo Hai off the coast of eastern China.

Escalation of Soviet naval patrols and further Soviet force infusions into the Northern Territories represent two predictable outcomes. But from the Japanese perspective, the costs are apparently offset as much by the political as well as economic security needs that bring the two nations together against the USSR.

Second, the fact that Japan shuns linkage politics in trade matters does not mean that she subscribes to the counter-proposition that "what is good for Japanese business is good for the country." Despite the USSR's position as a major Japanese trading partner, public opinion surveys since the early 1960s have consistently shown the Soviet Union leading the list as "the most disliked nation" (40 percent of all respondents in 1978) (USICA, 1979b: 2, 4). The PRC, by contrast, through frequently less important in purely economic terms, has always fared much better at the hands of the Japanese public. In 1978, only 10 percent of those surveyed regarded it as "most disliked," while 15 percent described it as the "most liked" (in contrast to under 5 percent for the USSR). Such findings indicate that the Japanese public does not regard the Communist bloc as a monolithic security threat. They also suggest that any efforts to restrict exports on such grounds would meet with little or no popular understanding.

There are other reasons as well why the national security issue has not figured more prominently in Japanese approaches to East-West trade and technology transfer. Many of these inhere in the dynamics of bureaucratic politics as they unfold in the Japanese setting. Although certain elements in the Ministry of Foreign Affairs have, at times, come out in favor of some sort of attempts at linkage (e.g., Japanese participation in the Tyumen project), they have been beaten down by opponents in the far more powerful MITI—and by the then-Foreign Minister Ohira himself (Curtis, 1977: 163-164).

Within this same perspective, it appears that linkage has no strong institutional supporter comparable to the Department of Defense in the United States. The Japanese counterpart, the JDA, appears less an autonomous bureaucracy than the arena for the play of interests centered variously in MITI, the Ministry of Finance, and the Ministry of Foreign Affairs. Until very recently, JDA position papers (the White Papers on defense) were drafted largely outside the agency and did not reflect an independent viewpoint. To judge by a recent White Paper, even the current JDA interest in improving Japan's security posture has been limited chiefly to demands for increased R&D expenditures for domestic production of military equipment. There is no mention of the strategic ramifications of technology transfer or the military implications of East-West trade (Japan Defense Agency, 1976: 128). Nor is there any parallel to the CTA that has occupied the attention of the U.S. Department of Defense. Rather, according to American Japan experts and Japanese scholars themselves, discussions of national security in that country continue to be dominated by three cardinal considerations on which all agree: (1) the USSR poses the chief military threat to Japan; (2) national security depends primarily on a sound defense relationship with the United States; and (3) the level of military threat from China is likely to be inconsequential for the foreseeable future regardless of Japanese initiatives. To this must be added a fourth consideration that frequently surfaced in our interviews, i.e., that Japanese assistance to the PRC to aid in her modernization will enhance Japanese security by reducing the probability of domestic upheavals and subsequent foreign policy radicalism on the part of forces on the mainland.

To the preceding reasons why U.S. effort to control technology transfer in the name of national security are likely to meet with opposition in Japan, we would add one final consideration. Japanese public opinion does not view security issues within the sort of "American mirror" that we frequently—and mistakenly—attribute to our partners in the alliance. According to the editor of the *Japan Economic Journal,* the consensus of Japanese public opinion is that monolithic security arrangements of the NATO type are inappropriate to Asia in general, whether they emanate from Moscow or Washington. Instead, security arrangements are best handled by "soft" structures—overlapping regional cooperation agreements in many forms without rigid security pacts (e.g., trade agreements, economic and political regional organizations, regional development banks) (Takayama, 1973). Thus, while the Japanese public in 1978 might manifest a much more favorable orientation toward defense expenditures and the Self-Defense Forces (SDF) than in the 1950s or 1960s, there is still no evident tendency to see security issues in mainly military terms (New York Times, 1979a; Tokuoda, 1979). A 1978 poll by the prime minister's Information Office demonstrated that although 86 percent of all respondents felt it was better to have the SDF than not, only 23 percent had a "good impression" of the SDF versus 53 percent who "did not have a bad impression" (USICA, 1979c: 2-3). Simultaneously, the vast majority (70 percent in 1975: 62 percent in 1978) felt that the SDF was of far more importance to disaster work or domestic order than to national security. Along similar lines, according to a December 1978 poll by the Japanese Public Opinion Survey Organization, most Japanese see "domestic political order" (47 percent) and the "state of the economy" (33 percent) as more critical to Japan's security than military measures or defense per se (14 percent) (USICA, 1979c: 7).

IV. JAPAN, COCOM, AND THE OPTIONS FOR U.S. EXPORT CONTROL POLICY

T he preceding analysis suggests that, viewed from Tokyo, U.S. moves to develop more stringent export controls on technology transfers from the West and to impose them on CoCom in the name of political, military, or even economic security for its member nations are likely to meet with an indifferent, if not openly hostile, response. No Japanese politician could support such moves without weakening his electoral base or, at a minimum, losing the support of vital interest groups within the Japanese business community. As Gordon Tubbs of the USICA (1979c: 7) observes, such a position is

> consistent with the belief expressed in many Japanese circles that maintaining friendly relations with all nations, establishing technological links between Japan and its neighbors (especially China and the Soviet Union) and extended economic assistance to raw materials producers ('resource diplomacy') are crucial means of protecting Japan's security.

It might appear, however, that the Soviet invasion of Afghanistan during the winter of 1979–1980 forced the Japanese into a radical reversal of their previous diplomatic stance and their foreign economic policy strategy. In February 1980, press reports in the United States suggested that Japan had at last bowed to U.S. pressure and that, stung by strong criticism for her failure to respond to Washington's calls for unity on the hostage issue in the Iranian crisis, Japan had agreed to cancel trade credits to the

USSR (New York Times, 1980a: 3; Boston Globe, 1980: 10). A careful analysis of the Japanese response, however, confirms the conclusions we have already drawn.

At the time of the Afghanistan crisis, Japan suspended but did not cancel credits for ongoing Siberian projects and others under negotiation. The affected projects included the Yakutia oil and natural gas exploration projects ($475 million), the Sakhalin offshore oil drilling project ($222.5 million), a rolled carbon steel project (jointly sponsored by Nippon Steel and Amco) ($350 million), and a new project to develop Siberian forestry resources ($500–$700 million) (Nihon Keizai Shimbun, 1980a: 1). Simultaneously, leading Japanese officials made it clear that the suspension was only temporary, that it did not affect private bank credits, and that it did not alter the basic Soviet-Japanese trade relationship significantly. In a speech to the Japanese Diet on February 7, Prime Minister Ohira stressed that Japanese participation in any Western embargo of technology shipments to the Soviet Union would depend upon prior West European and American initiatives. He thus reaffirmed Japan's traditional "wait-and-see" attitude and her preference for full consensus, rather than a "minimum winning coalition," within the alliance—a policy that so infuriates U.S. policymakers. A spokesman for the Japanese Chamber of Commerce and the Japanese-Soviet-East European trade association also emphasized that the postponement was temporary and would not affect the bilateral trade relationship between Japan and the USSR as an embargo might.

Although it is too soon for any firm conclusions, there is evidence to suggest that Japanese acquiescence to U.S. demands may have involved some rather complicated "horse trading." Shortly before Prime Minister Ohira's announcement, representatives of the Japanese business community were in Panama to consult with the U.S. Secretary of Commerce and the Panamanian government regarding Japanese participation in the construction of a second canal *and* Japanese-Soviet economic relations (Nihon Keizai Shimbun, 1980a: 1). Shortly after Ohira's announcement, the Japanese government also indicated a willingness to purchase some 1 million tons of American grain from the 17 million tons the Carter administration embargoed for sale to the Soviet Union (FBIS, 1980c: C5).

Opposition to the suspension of credits for the USSR quickly mounted within Japan and will probably weaken the government's already rather timid display of solidarity with the United States. The president of the Japan Economic Research Center, himself a former MITI official, denounced *any* form of sanctions against the USSR as "unworkable" and "counterproductive" for Japan (New York Times, 1980b: 8). On February 16, in an article entitled "Is It Beneficial to Japan?" Chief Cabinet Secretary Masayoshi Ito called the Japanese government's move a "cautious economic response" that stopped short of sanctions and had, as yet, no concrete form (Nihon Keizai Shimbun, 1980b: 1; FBIS, 1980c: C2-C3). Also in February of 1980, the influential paper *Nihon Keizai Shimbun* (1980c: 5) was already warning its readers that the government's political decision might have severe economic costs. It mentioned in particular Nippon Steel's potential loss of a highly profitable Soviet contract for 700 thousand tons of pipe for which a West German firm was also an active contender. The paper also pointed to negotiations between France and the USSR for new loans and trade credits and the Paris visit in mid-January of the Soviet deputy minister of foreign trade.

The Soviet response has been calculated to put pressure on Tokyo. On February 15, *Izvestia* announced that Moscow had warned Japan of its new, hard-line stance in the annual fisheries negotiations scheduled for late spring of 1980 (FBIS, 1980c: C3). At the same time, the USSR had made so many offers of new trade proposals—ranging from machine tools and weapons production equipment to communications components—that it seemed that the Kremlin did not take the Japanese show of unity with the United States too seriously.

It appears, therefore, that the Japanese response to U.S. demands for alliance solidarity in the wake of events in Afghanistan has been a continuation of the "omnidirectional" foreign policy of the Fukuda years (FBIS, 1980b: C3). Friendly relations with all nations, resource diversification, and trade links with both major Communist powers play just as important a role in 1980 as they did throughout the 1960s and 1970s. To date, Japan has temporized more than she has cooperated with U.S.

attempts to forge an alliance strategy. This is evident in the way in which MITI has cast the implementation of supposedly routine export control procedures (i.e., enforcement of CoCom control lists in the licensing of exports to the USSR) as "proof" of some kind of major shift in Japanese strategy. MITI has also promised to implement tighter screening of items in the CoCom "exceptions list" (i.e., controlled articles whose export Japan and other members can decide unilaterally)—but only if the United States and Western Europe make the first moves along such lines (FBIS, 1980a: C5). Meanwhile, the Japanese government has gone out of its way to avoid stirring up any anti-Soviet sentiment among the Japanese public. The prime minister moderated a statement by the new head of the JDA that called the Soviet Union an actual, rather than a "potential," threat and did not announce that three men arrested for spying had, in fact, passed JDA secrets to Soviet agents (FBIS, 1980a: C3). The public record shows that even in a crisis situation, Japan's foreign economic policy is geared less to an alliance strategy than to her traditional fear of being "defenseless on all sides."

Japanese behavior in the Afghanistan crisis should have been predicted by the United States, and there are deep-seated reasons why Japanese reactions in the future are likely to follow a similar pattern. U.S. efforts to tighten export controls within CoCom will probably weaken rather than reinforce the Western alliance. U.S. government sources report that Japanese businessmen are suspicious of American intentions in any moves designed to curb Japanese access to the China market for which they have labored long and assiduously over the past three decades. Indeed, the Japan-China Long-Term Trade Agreement of 1978 makes explicit reference (Article 2) to the fact that the "value of technology and industrial plants" to be exported from Japan to China shall be in the area of $7-8 billion, with the remaining $2-3 billion made up of construction materials, machinery, and equipment. Article 5 makes additional provision for "technological cooperation . . . in necessary fields of scientific technology" to implement the agreement and to expand economic exchanges (JPEW, 1978b: 1; International Energy, 1977: 15). Discussions between Prime Minister Ohira and Chinese Communist party Chairman Hua Guofeng, in December 1979 yielded agreement on a program whereby Japan will provide China with $1.5 billion in government credits for railway, port, and hydroelectric power projects over the next five to eight years (in addition to the $4 billion already furnished by Japanese private banks). Japanese steelmakers, electronics manufacturers, and the oil industry all expect to benefit handsomely from these arrangements that are expected to bolster the two-way trade exchange up to some $10 billion in 1980 (versus roughly $5 billion in 1978) (New York Times, 1979b and 1979c; and Table 2).

In return, according to the 1978 agreement, the Japanese are to receive some 47 million tons of Chinese crude oil (approximately 348 million barrels), about 12 percent of Japan's annual needs according to a Central Intelligence Agency projection for Japan in 1985. This will be spread over a five-year period, increasing from 6.8 million tons in 1978 to 15 million tons in 1982 (JPEW, 1978b). To be sure, this represents considerably less than Japan would have received under the now moribund Tyumen project (25 million tons a year). At the same time, such an agreement marks a small but important step in Japan's resource diversification strategy, as evinced by the fact that the Japanese government, to overcome the reluctance of the Japanese oil industry, has committed itself to providing aid to the latter to develop a $1.25 billion, 500 thousand barrels a day cracking facility specially designed to process the heavy, waxy Chinese oil. In addition, the government has committed $500 thousand to a feasibility study of a low-gravity cracking process (JPEW, 1978a: 6).

Thus, any controls that impede Japan's planned transfer to the PRC of oil and coal production equipment, petrochemical plants, harbor facilities, or the like will not meet with a favorable response in Tokyo. This is true in view of the long-term shift in the structure of Japanese exports to the PRC that the agreement lays out. It also holds in terms of the sizeable increments in total trade volume—over $20 billion over time in addition to current levels—that the agreement promises for the future (JPEW, 1978b: 2).

From another perspective, more stringent export controls and an expanded CoCom list represent a further intrusion of trade policy (or "low foreign policy") into "high foreign policy" issues. The chief advantage in separating the two is that it shields foreign policy from the excessive intrusion of domestic, economic, partisan interests through the trade policy channel. Once particularistic pressures come to the fore, international trading rules and GATT provisions will be visibly weakened. Protection rather than free trade might emerge as the order of the day, whatever the de jure provisions might be (Cooper, 1973: 46-47).

In more concrete terms, trade policies, if considered in isolation, can sour foreign policy generally, and can lead to configurations in international relations that are rather different from those which American "high foreign policy" strategies might dictate. It may at some point be necessary to decide whether or not the advantages to the American political economy of retarding Soviet technological development by some three to five years is really worth the price of the political ill will such moves could cause among U.S. allies, especially Japan. It is certainly worth reminding ourselves, as the editor of *Japan Economic Journal* pointed out in 1972, that the Japanese have long believed that U.S. trade policies toward Japan were based on considerable misperceptions, unfair charges, and, above all, excessive interference by domestic lobbies in matters that quite properly should be considered on their own merits (Takayama, 1973: 5-21). In such an atmosphere, U.S. efforts to develop a CoCom consensus on new controls are more likely to generate increased acrimony rather than agreement.

In fairness to the U.S. position, it is also important to point out that current Japanese trading practices with the Communist world may threaten the international economic and political order as much as any efforts to curtail technology transfer. This is due less to actual transfers, however, than to the structure of such trade itself. The 1978 OECD report warned that current tendencies in East-West trade that pull in the direction of bilateralism, counterpurchase agreements, and barter deals must be viewed with trepidation. Here Japan appears a major, though hardly the only, offender. The report observes that such deals contribute little to the freer flow of trade on a truly multilateral basis. They also contravene the ideal of an open trading system on which the GATT arrangements are based. Ultimately, such trade will encourage the development of a number of cul-de-sacs. Communist bloc exports will be limited by the fact that "potential exports of energy products and raw materials are restricted both by the amount of capital necessary to increase production [in the West as well as the East] and by the capacity of Western markets to absorb them" (OECD, 1978: 334).

Bilateralism is also disadvantageous from a political standpoint. It does little to promote "the reciprocal adjustment between economic structures in the East and West" (OECD, 1978: 335). It merely postpones the day when Communist states might adjust their economic systems to provide more manufactured goods for their own consumers and nonmilitary use. It also prevents trade linkages from having any larger political, social, or strategic impact in such economies. Last but not least, it obscures the need for a head-on approach to the steadily worsening debt situation in Communist states, while setting an unfortunate precedent for the LDCs in their trade relations with the West. If counterpurchase is acceptable for the USSR and PRC, why not for Africa, Latin America, and South Asia as well?

In view of the dynamic described by the preceding chapters, a convincing case can be made for progressive Japanese disillusionment with CoCom and increasing resistance over time to the constraints it poses. Unfortunately, given the classified nature of information regarding CoCom violations, it is impossible for an outside observer to argue the case on the basis of hard evidence. Interviews suggest that the Japanese to date still accept the "rolling technological embargo" principle that, according to the British economist Peter Wiles, underlies the whole CoCom edifice (Wiles, 1976: 35). But they appear to have done so with a vengeance. If, indeed, such an embargo (in Wiles's terms) is nothing but an extention of the desire to maintain a technological gap *"just as every individual corporation in the high technology sector tries to do,"* then in Japanese eyes only the most minimal government intervention may be necessary.

From the Japanese perspective, other factors may also be at work undermining the CoCom consensus. Japan's economic recovery has generated new areas of competition with other Western nations, especially in areas where U.S. goods and technology have been predominant (e.g., large computers). If Japan believes CoCom decisions are largely for the benefit of American corporations, rather than based on strategic calculations, resistance will probably intensify. Meanwhile, growing Western protectionism against Japanese goods (e.g., the "escape clause" of the 1974 U.S. trade act), coupled with import restrictions now arising in Western Europe, may make the Communist bloc increasingly important as a market for Japanese exports (MITI, 1978d: 16-17).

The depressed state of Japan's shipbuilding industry and its severely underutilized capacity may already incline certain Japanese firms to push for a relatively more liberal government approach toward the export of maritime vessels with possible military application. Japanese firms as a whole have made a major contribution to the aggregate tonnage of the Soviet merchant fleet, as well as contributing to an increase in the mean size of its vessels—one indicator of a successful naval modernization program (Mathieson, 1979: 187-196). (As American naval strategists frequently note, a major Soviet concern is to provide for rapid conversion of its merchant marine to military purposes.) Under such circumstances, "floating dock" cases may become more, rather than less, frequent.

Such factors, when combined with a diminished American presence in Asia and Japanese rapprochement with the PRC, sooner or later may mean that traditional American arguments for bolstering security arrangements through trade controls will ring with little conviction. At the same time, increased Japanese self-reliance in defense matters appears one prediction of the early 1970s that has come true (Morley, 1972). This reliance will eventually engender an increased R&D effort to develop a home-grown weapons technology and an adequate production base. Western experience shows that under such circumstances, the impulse to recoup investments through the sale of related products quickly becomes quite strong. How compatible this impulse will be with CoCom restrictions, especially since other CoCom members no longer face similar start-up pressures, remains to be seen.

We do know that Japan's business community, particularly the Japan Federation of Employers Organizations, has traditionally been more hawkish on defense spending and weapons production (among other things, as a source of new technology spin off for civilian industry) than have the politicians and public at large (Langdon, 1972: 115-117, 133). And, according to Langdon, "the arms makers [in Japan] continue to look longingly at overseas sales." The first requests for export licenses were tended in the early 1970s. Since a national debate on defense spending, arms exports, and Japan's total dependence on the United States for its security was initiated by a speech by former Prime Minister Takeo Fukuda in the Diet in January 1978, such pressures can only increase (Scott-Stokes, 1979: 19).

All the same, it is far too early to speculate that the balance will shift decisively in the direction just described. A number of countervailing factors still exist whose combined, centripetal force promises to maintain existing CoCom arrangements intact. Whether or not such forces are adequate to sustain any U.S. attempts to strengthen the consensus is more debatable.

Chief among these forces is what one respondent described as a strong Japanese policy sentiment against exporting arms, nuclear weapons, or anything of obvious military significance. Such sentiments, rooted as they are in the postwar psychology of leaders and masses alike, are reinforced continually by pragmatic considerations. Asian nations, which in 1977 accounted for fully 33 percent of Japan's export market and over 50 percent of her imported commodities, would react both economically and politically to any signs of revived Japanese militarism or other elements of a Greater East Asia Co-Prosperity Sphere. CoCom or no, Japan probably cannot afford to export militarily relevant products. The restraints imposed on any export mix by Japan's own history may mitigate opposition to CoCom restrictions.

A case can also be made that CoCom is useful to Japan in a variety of ways. In the face of possible increased pressure from China to tilt in her direction, especially after the Japanese agreed to include an antihegemony clause in their peace treaty, CoCom policies could provide the Japanese with a welcome respite. They fit well into Japan's widely publicized efforts to develop a policy of even-handedness in dealing with her two powerful Communist neighbors. If the PRC or the Soviet Union should pressure Japan to sell ships, aircraft, or machinery with strategic significance, the CoCom list provides an inoffensive and unchallengeable rationale for a refusal.

Second, the Japanese still have genuine concerns about Soviet policy. If we are to judge by Prime Minister Ohira's statements on the eve of his visit to the United States in May 1979, Japanese leaders have become increasingly concerned about the USSR's military posture in the Far East (New York Times, 1979e). The Northern Territories have taken on increased strategic as well as economic importance in the eyes of both parties to the dispute, as Peggy Falkenheim has pointed out (Falkenheim, 1977). Despite their principled refusal to use trade for political leverage, successive Japanese governments have refused to enter into the kinds of long-term trade commitments that the Soviets have been urging on them. Further, according to Soviet sources, the Japanese have been dragging their heels in implementing an intergovernmental agreement on scientific and technical exchanges. Although the agreement was signed in 1974, it still had not been implemented in 1978 (Stoliarov and Khesin, 1977: 252–253).

It is also possible that CoCom arrangements may be supported simply because no effective domestic political opposition has yet appeared. However influential prodefense sentiments may be among certain segments of the business community, it remains to be seen whether they will eventually capture the "commanding heights" of the *Keidanren* leadership (the umbrella organization of the Japanese business community) or that of the Liberal Democratic party. Despite the generally pro-Soviet stance of the Japanese Communist party (at least historically), it must be balanced against the anti-Soviet posture of the Japanese Socialists (Swearingen, 1978: 117). Both parties insist on an improvement in political relations, i.e., territorial concessions on the Northern Territories, prior to any major diplomatic rapprochement or long-term economic agreement. Meanwhile, the consensual facade of what Chalmers Johnson (1978) describes as "Japan's public

policy companies" has not yet given way to bickering and recrim-
inations about trade policy—at least that outsiders can hear. It
may well be that for every company division head who is
enthusiastic about larger equipment sales to the USSR or China,
there is a products division chief who gently reminds his bosses
that sales today will mean the loss of markets tomorrow. If this is
indeed the case, then the apparent silence of the Japanese business community on CoCom becomes explicable.

The Japanese position on export controls, while laced through
with a number of uncertainties and contradictions, as yet does
not seem to be on a collision course with current American
policy. By the same token, there is little or no sympathy with
tighter controls over either end products or technology. The
Japanese position is neither more nor less "correct" than the
position of those in the United States who are concerned about
diminishing Western technological advantage. The Japanese position does, however, underscore an irony. By 1979, Japan—the
land of strong executive government, a quasi-governmental and
highly centralized trading structure, and a tradition of close ties
between the military and business establishments—has emerged as
a leading advocate of free trade, minimal control of exports, and
trade-according-to-comparative advantage. Adam Smith would
heartily approve (Calleo and Rowland, 1973: 210–219). But
Japan has done so chiefly with respect to the Communist world—
to which it is nevertheless opposed on social, economic, military,
and political grounds. Perhaps *Alice in Wonderland* metaphors are
appropriate to the subject matter after all.

In light of such a situation, it is important to emphasize that
American options for limiting technology transfers from the West
to the Communist bloc are not eliminated, merely altered. As
Chalmers Johnson has pointed out in another context vis-à-vis
Japan, our allies may feel that U.S. technology transfer policy
pays too much attention to legal matters (e.g., CoCom regulations) and too little attention to economics (Johnson, 1978:
225). From this perspective, first of all, *efforts to alter, reinforce,
or replace the CoCom structure must focus on the domestic
economic exigencies confronted by each of the governments*

involved, not on those of the United States alone. Strategic issues should not be considered in isolation, as the CTA of the Department of Defense seems to recommend.

Second, *decisions regarding CoCom should be made in the context of a broad-based, multidimensional assessment of the nature of the Western alliance, with particular attention to the political and economic, as well as military, factors.* In the case of Japan, this means a recognition that U.S. interests would suffer severely, globally as well as regionally, if Japan were to fall to a hostile government, or under one that would detach it from the existing international trading system because of poorly conceived American pressures (Johnson and Yager, 1978: 3). Some priority must be assigned to cooperation per se, so that U.S. and Japanese policies can be coordinated in trade and technology transfer as well as in military-strategic planning. To insure such cooperation requires a skillful rather than heavy-handed use of our position as Japan's primary trading partner. Above all, the United States must avoid tilting the balance by advocating trading policies that might threaten the Japanese way of life. Economic warfare that threatens Japan domestically might even be considered as much of a threat to Japan as military aggression by the Communist states (Swearingen, 1978: 208–209).

Third, *alternative ways to regulate technology transfer outside of CoCom should be explored.* In the case of Japan, this might take the form of more joint development ventures within the Communist bloc, such as the Tyumen oil fields project and the Sakhalin continental shelf project, both involving American companies. Japanese rhetoric concerning an "autonomous foreign policy" notwithstanding, the history of the Tyumen project reveals that the Japanese were both willing and anxious to develop an "American connection." This was to be used not merely to spread the economic risk but also to have an American counterweight in the event that Soviet military or political pressures were brought to bear once the project was underway (Curtis, 1977: 171–172). Moreover, it is easier to hammer out agreements on what technologies should or should not be traded if all nations involved have a more or less equal stake in the outcome. The PRC (and perhaps Eastern Europe) also finds U.S. involvement attractive, for it sees U.S. participation as a counterweight to any attempts by the USSR to bring pressure on Western nations separately.

One instance where Japan is successfully involved in such a framework involves the Sakhalin oil development project, a joint Soviet-Japanese venture managed by SODECO (Sakhalin Oil Development Cooperation Company) and scheduled to run until 1982. In October 1977, the first four test wells drilled off the coast of Sakhalin were producing 2,500 barrels of oil daily of a quality considerably better than what the Chinese have to offer Japan (New York Times, 1977; JPEW, 1977: 1). One U.S. company, Gulf Oil, publicly participates in the project both as an equity shareholder in SODECO (3.82 percent) and as a provider of oil rigs, high speed drill bits, and technical expertise. Political as well as economic considerations seem to have influenced the Japanese invitation to Gulf. Furthermore, according to U.S. government sources and from information on Japanese overseas petroleum producers, it is likely that other "Japanese" oil company participants are, in fact, subsidiaries (wholly or partially owned) of American interests (JPEW, 1977: 2; Japan National Committee, 1978: 9-13). In any event, Japanese oil executives admit that they will be turning to U.S. companies for the technology involved in seismic analysis, recording equipment, drill bits, and rigs for many years to come. A larger number of such bilateral or multilateral schemes involving several Western powers in Communist economic development means that technology transfer could be regulated through the coordinated national mechanisms of the individual partners rather than through an international forum such as CoCom.

U.S. technology transfer policy needs to be formulated in terms of the broadest costs/benefits analysis possible. Insofar as we desire to restrict our allies in the export of those technologies that we consider strategic, the real issue is not the effectiveness or speed of the mechanisms involved. The issue is what price the United States (and Congress) is willing to pay—and how expensive such restrictions might be in terms of both the broader political alliance and of domestic forces within the United States. Japanese compliance with new international export controls may exact a price that requires us to live a little longer—or more graciously— with what the Department of Commerce has labeled "Japan, Inc." (If this is indeed a misnomer, the U.S. sacrifice may not be all that great.) More specifically, the United States may have to provide its Japanese partner with economically compelling reasons for pursuing our political strategy toward the Communist bloc rather than their own. For example, there should be discussion of the sale of Alaskan oil to Japan to lessen their dependency on Communist bloc suppliers. At present this is forbidden by Congressional mandate. Simultaneously, the United States could soften the potential impact of whatever technology transfer might take place between Japan and the USSR or the PRC through American participation in various joint development ventures. There could also be intelligent and extensive discussion among those concerned with technology transfer or the implementation of a CTA as to whether it is more in our national interest to restrict Japanese initiatives in technology transfers to the Communist world or to institute orderly marketing arrangements to regulate and restrict Japanese trade with the United States. It is unlikely that the fabric of the alliance can be strengthened by efforts to pursue both goals simultaneously, although this appears to represent U.S. strategy at present.

The natural tendency of policymakers is to sidestep such thorny issues. The solutions are admittedly difficult ones, and the domestic political costs to U.S. decision makers could be large. But the evidence is that the United States cannot ignore the issue any more than can its Japanese (or German or French or British) counterpart (Yergin, 1980). To develop an effective policy for regulating technology transfer *and* for strengthening the Western alliance, Congress should devote more attention to trade-offs and to the political and economic considerations of all parties involved—not just those of the United States. In technology transfer policies, as in foreign policy in general, the United States is no longer unchallenged. Trade policies formulated without taking this into account, whatever their short-run attractiveness, are short sighted and will prove counterproductive.

Notes

1. Portions of the research for this paper were used in *Technology and East-West Trade* (Office of Technology Assessment, 1979). This paper, however, reflects the views of the author and in no way represents those of the Office of Technology Assessment, United States Congress.

2. Similar sentiments were expressed by Mr. Hatoyama, Minister of Foreign Affairs, in a speech to the Diet in October 1977. According to the strategy he outlined for Japanese-Soveit relations in 1978, Japan would strive to develop relations across a number of fronts—economic, cultural, and political—simultaneously. Japan would insist only that any long-term relations depend on a peace treaty and a settlement of the territorial issue (Foreign Press Center, 1977). A similar "unlinking" of trade and political issues was evident in the presentation of Foreign Minister Samoda to the Diet a year later, in September 1978 (Foreign Press Center, 1978: 6-7).

References

An Analysis of Export Control of U.S. Technology–A DOD Perspective (1976). A Report of the Defense Science Board Task Force on the Export of U.S. Technology. Washington, D.C.: Office of the Director of Defense Research and Engineering, DOD (February 4). (Known as the Bucy Report).

BAKER, R. and R. BOHLIG (1967) "The Control of Exports: A Comparison of the Law of the United States, Canada, Japan and the FRG." The International Lawyer 1: 163–191.

BINGHAM, J. B. and V. C. JOHNSON (1979) "A Rational Approach to Export Controls." Foreign Affairs 57, 2 (Spring): 894-920.

BLAKER, M. (1977) "Probe, Push and Panic: the Japanese Tactical Style in International Negotiations," pp. 55-102 in Robert Scalapino (ed.) The Foreign Policy of Modern Japan. Berkeley: University of California Press.

Boston Globe (1980) (February 8): 10.

BRUSH, P. N. (1971) "Implementation of the Export Administration Act of 1969." Connecticut Law Review 4,1 (Summer): 35-53.

CALLEO, D. P. and B. M. ROWLAND (1973) America and the World Political Economy. Bloomington: Indiana University Press.

CARRICK, R. J. (1978) East-West Technology Transfer in Perspective. Policy Papers in International Affairs, Number 9. Berkeley: University of California Press.

COOPER, R. N. (1973) "Trade Policy is Foreign Policy," pp. 46-64 in Richard N. Cooper (ed.) A Reordered World: Emerging International Economic Problems. Washington, DC: Potomac Associates.

CRAWFORD, SIR J. and S. OKITA (eds.) (1978) Raw Materials and Pacific Economic Integration. Vancouver: University of British Columbia Press.

CURTIS, G. L. (1977) "The Tiumen Oil Development Project and Japanese Foreign Policy Decision Making," pp. 147-74 in Robert Scalapino (ed.) The Foreign Policy of Modern Japan. Berkeley: University of California Press.

DAVIS, R. M. (1979) The Department of Defense's Statement on Critical Technologies for Export Control. Prepared for the Subcommittee on International Economic Policy and Trade, Committee on Foreign Affairs, House of Representatives, 96th Congress, First Session (March 22).

ECKHARDT, W. and R. WHITE (1971) "A Test of the Mirror-Image Hypothesis," pp. 308-317 in Erik P. Hoffman and Frederick J. Fleron, Jr. (eds.) The Conduct of Soviet Foreign Policy. New York: Aldine.

The Economist (1979a) "Tokyo Takes Heart." 270, 7073 (March 24): 106-07.

——— (1979b) "Rising Exports Again This Year." 271, 7081 (May 19): 88.

——— (1979c) "It'll All Come All Right One Day." 272, 7096 (September 1): 68.

——— (1979d) "Russian Hopes, Japanese Doubts." 272, 7099 (September 22): 86.

——— (1979e) "Japan and China: Aid Precedes Trade." 273, 7110 (December 8): 71-72.

——— (1979f) "China's Question, Russia's Question." 273, 7113 (December 29): 17-34.

FALKENHEIM, P. L. (1977) "Some Determining Factors in Soviet-Japanese Relations." Pacific Affairs 50,4 (Winter): 604-609.

FBIS (Foreign Broadcast Information Service, Daily Reports: Asia and Pacific) (1980a) IV, 029 (February 11): C5.

——— (1980b) IV, 030 (February 12): C3.

——— (1980c) IV, 034 (February 19): C2-C5.

FLERON, F. J., Jr. (1977) "The Western Connection: Technical Rationality and Soviet Politics." Soviet Union 4, 1: 58-84.Foreign Press Center (1977) Speech by Itchiro Hatoyama, Minister of Foreign Affairs. Tokyo: Foreign Press Center (October 3).

——— (1978) Foreign Policy Address. Tokyo: Foreign Press Center (September 20).

GERSHMAN, C. (1979) "Selling Them the Rope: Business and the Soviets." Commentary 67, 4 (April): 35-46.

GOLDMAN, M. I. (1976) "U.S. Policies on Technology Sales to the USSR," pp. 103−118 in East-West Technological Cooperation. Brussels: NATO Directorate of Economic Affairs.

HANSON, P. (1976) "The Diffusion of Imported Technology in the USSR," pp. 143−164 in East-West Technological Cooperation. Brussels: NATO Directorate of Economic Affairs.

——— (1978) "Western Technology in the Soviet Economy." Problems of Communism 17 (November-December): 20−30.

HARDT, J. P., G. HOLLIDAY and Y. C. KIM (1974) Western Investment in Communist Economies. Washington, D.C.: Government Printing Office.

HUNTINGTON, S. P. (1978) "Address," pp. 7-26 in Integrating National Security and Trade Policy. West Point: United States Military Academy.

The International Energy Situation: Outlook for 1985 (1977) Washington, D.C.: Government Printing Office.

Japan Defense Agency (1976) The Defense of Japan. Tokyo: Japan Defense Agency.

Japanese National Committee of the World Petroleum Congresses (1978) The Petroleum Industry in Japan, 1977. Tokyo: Japanese National Committee of the World Petroleum Congresses.

JETRO (Japanese External Trade Organization) (1972) How to Approach the China Market. Tokyo: Press International.

——— (1977) Japan's Plant Exports, Number 11. Tokyo: JETRO.

——— (1978) Japan's Import System. Tokyo: JETRO.

JOHNSON, C. (1977) "MITI and Japanese International Economic Policy," pp. 281-318 in Robert Scalapino (ed.) The Foreign Policy of Modern Japan. Berkeley: University of California Press.

——— (1978) Japan's Public Policy Companies. Washington, D.C.: American Enterprise Institute for Public Policy Research.

JOHNSON, S. and J. A. YAGER (1978) The Military Equation in Northeast Asia. Washington, D.C.: Brookings Institution.

JPEW (Japan Petroleum and Energy Weekly) (1977) 1, 2, 43 (October 24).

——— (1978a) (January 16): 3, 13.

——— (1978b) (February 13): 7, 13.

KIMURA, H. (1979) Cultural Problems in Soviet-Japanese Fishing Negotiations. Unpublished paper delivered at the East-West Institute, Hawaii.

KITAGAWA, T. (1972) "Legal Aspects of Soviet-Japanese Trade." Law and Contemporary Problems 37, 4 (Autumn): 557-570.

KOJIMA, K. (1977) Japan and a New World Economic Order. Boulder: Westview Press.

KOSAKA, M. (1977) "The International Economic Policy of Japan," pp. 207-226 in Robert Scalapino (ed.) The Foreign Policy of Modern Japan. Berkeley: University of California Press.

KRAVALIS, H., A. J. LENZ, H. RAFFEL, and J. YOUNG (1979) "Quantification of Western Exports of High Technology Products to Communist Countries," pp. 34-55 in Issues in East-West Commercial Relations. A Compendium of Papers Submitted to the Joint Economic Committee, Congress of the United States. Washington, D.C.: Government Printing Office.

LANGDON, F. (1972) "The Attitude of the Business Community," pp. 111-134 in James William Morley (ed.) Forecast for Japan: Security in the 1970s. Princeton: Princeton University Press.

LEE, C-J. (1976) Japan Faces China: Political and Economic Relations in the Post-War Era. Baltimore: Johns Hopkins Press.

MATHIESON, R. (1979) Japan's Role in Soviet Economic Growth: Transfer of Technology Since 1965. New York: Praeger Publishers.

MITI (Ministry of International Trade and Industry) (1970) Tsusho hakusho soron. Tokyo: MITI.

———— (1973) Tsusho hakusho soron. Tokyo: MITI.
——— (1976) Tsusho hakusho soron. Tokyo: MITI.
——— (1977) Tsusho hakusho soron. Tokyo: MITI.
——— (1978a) Export Control: Export Trade Control Order. Tokyo: MITI.
——— (1978b) Summary Report, Trade of Japan, No. 10. Tokyo: MITI.
——— (1978c) Summary Report, Trade of Japan, No. 1f. Tokyo: MITI.
——— (1978d) White Paper on International Trade, Japan, 1978: Summary. Tokyo: MITI.
MORLEY, J. W. (1972) "Economics and Balanced Defense," pp. 9-34 in James William Morley (ed.) Forecast for Japan: Security in the 1970s. Princeton: Princeton University Press.
New York Times (1977) "Russia and Japan Report Discovery of Sakhalin Oil Field." (October 13).
——— (1979a) "U.S. Sees Japan Improving Defense." (November 11).
——— (1979b) "Ohira Leaves for Visit to Peking." (December 5).
——— (1979c) "Japan-China Meeting Strengthening Economic Ties." (December 9).
——— (1979d) "Japan Goal: Lead in Computers." (December 12).
——— (1979e) "Japan's Premier Warns of Soviet Aggression." (April 20).
——— (1980a) "Japan Facing Complex Policy Issue About Sanctions." (January 19).
——— (1980b) "Pandas, Symbol of the Wooing of the Japanese." (February 24).
Nihon Keizai Shimbun (1980a) (February 8): 1.
——— (1980b) (February 16): 1.
——— (1980c) (February 21): 5.
Nippon: A Chartered Survey of Japan, 1978 (1978) Tokyo: Kokusei-sha.
Nisso To-o Bo'ekikai (1959) Nisso Bo'eki Yoron. Tokyo: Nisso To-o Bo' ekikai Jimukiuku.
——— (1978) Nisso Bo'eki Yoron. Tokyo: Nisso To-o Bo'ekikai Jimukiuku.
OECD (Organization for Economic Cooperation and Development) [1978] Technology Transfer Between East and West. SPT (77) 16, First Revision. Paris: OECD.
Office of Technology Assessment, Congress of the United States (1979) Technology and East-West Trade. Washington, D.C.: Government Printing Office.
OGAWA, K. (1979) "Economic and Trade Relations Between Japan and the Soviet Union, China, and the Socialist Countries of Europe." Unpublished monograph for the Japanese Association for Trade with the Soviet Union and the Socialist Countries of Europe. Tokyo.
OHKAWA, K. and H. ROSOVSKY (1973) Japanese Economic Growth: Trend Acceleration in the Twentieth Century. Stanford: Stanford University Press.
Outline of the White Paper on Science and Technology (1977) Tokyo: Foreign Press Center.

PODOLSKI, T. (1976) "Evolution of East-West Technological Transfer," pp. 119–143 in East-West Technological Cooperation. Brussels: NATO Directorate of Economic Affairs.

ROBINSON, T. W. (1978) "Thoughts on Siberian Development and Its Implications for the Possible Roles Therein of Japan and the United States." Paper presented at Airlie House Conference on Siberia.

SCOTT-STOKES, H. (1979) "It's All Right to Talk Defense Again in Japan." New York Times Magazine (February 11).

SILK, L. (1979) "How Japan Sees the China Market." New York Times, (May 18).

STOLIAROV, I. S. and E. S. KHESIN (1977) Iaponiia v sisteme mirovykh khoziastvennykh sviazei. Moscow: Nauka.

SWEARINGEN, R. (1978) The Soviet Union and Post-War Japan: Escalating Challenge and Response. Stanford: Hoover Institution.

TAKAYAMA, Y. (1973) "Don't Take Japan for Granted," pp. 1–21 in Richard N. Cooper (ed.) A Reordered World: Emerging International Economic Problems. Washington, D.C.: Potomac Associates.

TERADA, Y. (1972) "System of Trade Between Japan and Eastern Europe, including the Soviet Union." Law and Contemporary Problems 37, 3 (Summer): 431–436.

TOKUODA, T. (1979) "Japan–Red or Dead?" New York Times (September 2).

U.S., Department of Commerce (1979a) China's Economy and Foreign Trade, 1978-79. Washington, D.C.: Government Printing Office.

––– (1979b) "IW Exports to the USSR." Computerized tables.

USICA (U.S. International Communication Agency) (1979a) Research Memorandum (April 24).

––– (1979b) Foreign Opinion Notes (May 7).

––– (1979c) Research Memorandum (April 27).

Vneshnaia torgovlia SSSR v 1977 godu. Statisticheskii sbornik (1978) Moscow: Statistika.

WILES, P. (1976) "On the Prevention of Technology Transfer," pp. 23–42 in East-West Technological Cooperation. Brussels: NATO Directorate of Economic Affairs.

YASHIKI, H. (1964) Nitchu Bo'eki Anai. Tokyo: Nikon-kei zai Shinbunsha.

YERGIN, A. S. (1980) East-West Technology Transfers: European Perspectives. The Washington Papers, No. 75. Beverly Hills: SAGE Publications.

YOUNG, A. K. (1979) The Sogo Shosha: Japan's Multi-National Trading Companies. Boulder: Westview Press.